Wait, Beloved, for Darkness's Gift

Letha C. Chamberlain

PublishAmerica
Baltimore

At the specific preference of the author, PublishAmerica allowed this work to remain exactly as the author intended, verbatim, without editorial input.

ISBN: 1-4241-8262-X
PUBLISHED BY PUBLISHAMERICA, LLLP
www.publishamerica.com
Baltimore

Printed in the United States of America

To all those who read this poetry while in darkness:

You are showing this lowly wrench how to pray incessantly,
O Lord of My Heart. Once in pain and agony—now these crosses
Have become for me great joy and peacefulness…
Through the darkness You have given me I have found that You
Reward the Ground I walk upon—with firm and friendly
Carrying of the burdens I shoulder. O Jesus, You Who
Are that Ground so sound and strong! Be Thou steel
That certains me for this life I lead…I love the very
Breath that breathes me to eternity! You are Beauty,
Truth, and Love for us humankind—make us Thine!
And guide the souls who are weary of life's exigencies.
Give them courage to meet the challenges interiorly,
So they learn to know You as Your loving Majesty.
This I wish for them—so grant it, if it be Your Will…
That they, too, have the joy of being with You filled.
I love them, too, dear Lord, and hope they have the best,
And for them there is peace and happiness in Your rest.
It is only there found—on this magnificent God-quest.

Wait, Beloved, for Darkness's Gift

Part I...

The Psalms in Haiku from the New Jerusalem Translation of the Holy Bible

Part II...

Meditations for the Occasions of Your Life
These are 59 short meditations originally written as "spiritual bouquets" to be given with prayers and good deeds for events in the lives of Catholic parishioners. These can be given for that purpose or used to deepen one's spiritual walk with God in everyday life celebrations, crises, and ordinary happenings in brief, thoughtful meditations written by a spiritual director/catechist/contemplative.

A Wedding
A Birth of a Baby
On Illness
On the Loss of a Child
The Baptism of a Baby
After the Easter Vigil—for the Neophyte
Confirmation—for Adults

Part III...

Prayer-Poems written in the year 2006-2007 on the theme of mainly love-psalms and those to be shared with others.

Part I

The Psalms in Haiku from the
New Jerusalem Translation of the Holy Bible

Psalm 1...

The good are like trees
Planted in rich soil; not the
Sinful who die mean...

Psalm 2...

God's anointed son...
All hail with heavenly might!
We may take refuge.

Psalm 3...

Countless enemies
Destroy teeth and face, my shield...
God will rescue me!

Psalm 4...

In You is my rest...
Yahweh, Worker of Wonders!
I sleep securely.

Psalm 5...

In reverence, yield!
Yahweh, my savior, my shield...
I rejoice in You!

Psalm 6...

O save me, Great Lord!
Protect me from those who harm,
For their wiles alarm.

Psalm 7...

Judge me—O Just One!
You who are shield and refuge...
I sing praise to You.

Psalm 8...

Poor man—near divine,
In what works God has revealed
His magnificence!

Psalm 9-10...

Oh! So orderly...
God avenges the evil
Man has wrought on man!

Psalm 11...

Uprightness is blessed!
Yahweh in His holy house
Scrutinizes us...

Psalm 12...

Yahweh's promises...
Silver seven times refined.
Man's lips boast and sigh.

Psalm 13...

I demand answers,
O Lord, for my longing heart,
So I sing again.

Psalm 14...

They are in exile
And deny their God—One Just.
Upright they come home.

Psalm 15...

God, to dwell with You
On Your high, holy mountain
We must live truly.

Psalm 16…

Protect me, O God!
Delightful Inheritance…
You are happiness!

Psalm 17…

I have done no wrong.
Shelter me against attack;
Lord, this song so strong…

Psalm 18…

Yahweh's faithful love,
Anointed heirs of David,
Bleeding with men's blood…

Psalm 19…

God's precepts are Law…
As it courses hot and true,
The sun rises forth.

Psalm 20…

May Yahweh grant you
Help from the sanctuary…
King: sacrificer…

Psalm 21...

We kings have no pow'r
Save Yahweh—O'erarching One.
He gives us splendor.

Psalm 22...

My God, O my God,
Why have You forsaken me?
but You will fulfill.

Psalm 23...

By my Shepherd led
Through green and dark passages...
I am oiled and fed.

Psalm 24...

Yahweh Sabaoth,
He is the King of glory.
Seek His high mountain!

Psalm 25...

Ransom Israel!
God, there are many troubles,
For You I name all...

Psalm 26...

Pity me, my God!
Judge me, since I am blameless;
I give you my laud.

Psalm 27...

Let your heart be bold!
So the wicked stumble/fall...
Put your hope in God!

Psalm 28...

Yahweh hears your cries
When you call Him. Deny...sink
To oblivion.

Psalm 29...

Give Yahweh His due...
Convulsing, thundering strength
Brings glorious peace.

Psalm 30...

Yahweh—turn Your face—
I am terrified! Turn here—
Dawning cries of joy!

Psalm 31...

Lord, You heard my plea
Made with hurt, in misery...
I hope in Yahweh.

Psalm 32...

I confess my guilt...
You forgave my heavy sins...
With God I am filled!

Psalm 33...

Rely on His love;
Yahweh watches over us.
Let hope rest above.

Psalm 34...

In all due order...
Yahweh delights for the good.
Proclaim His Greatness.

Psalm 35...

I am so attacked,
I worry restlessly; but...
God wills perfect peace.

Psalm 36...

Sin in depths of heart?
Those who seek God see the light...
Wicked wander far...

Psalm 37...

In God's good order...
Righteous live to serve in peace...
Wicked get penance.

Psalm 38...

Lord, I am so wrong...
Your indignation presses.
Be my guiding song.

Psalm 39...

But a puff of wind—
(You gaze upon me: a breath)
You are Holy Lord.

Psalm 40...

Though my sins o'erwhelm,
Yahweh, my rock, comes to aid...
Tender, His love saves.

Psalm 41...

Yahweh, have pity!
Though I am sick, they leave me...
But God, I praise Thee!

Psalm 42-43...

I thirst for You, God—
have no food but mournful tears...
Yet I hope in You.

Psalm 44...

Victory was Yours,
O Lord, in antiquity.
What happened today?

Psalm 45...

Feast, royal wedding...
O man of God's anointing—
Praise—with God's woman!

Psalm 46...

Yahweh Sabaoth,
Our citadel, is with us—
The God of Jacob...

Psalm 47…

Yahweh, the Most High—
Great King over all the world—
Let the music sound!

Psalm 48…

Your Zion, O God,
Trembling on the mountain-top
Praises Your Kingship!

Psalm 49…

Hear this, all nations!
When rich, people lose good sense—
They are like dumb beasts.

Psalm 50…

Let yourself know this;
Thanksgiving is sacrifice
Pleasing to our God.

Psalm 51…

Have mercy on me,
O God, in Your tenderness…
I grievously sin.

Psalm 52...

Your pride in evil
Will but come to certain end.
I trust in the Lord.

Psalm 53...

No vile one does right
And fools say, "There is no God."
But He brings us home...

Psalm 54...

God, hear my prayer...
Save me from all my troubles—
I give sacrifice...

Psalm 55...

Men with bad intent
Seek to do me wrong, O God...
I trust still in You.

Psalm 56...

By the vows I make—
Though some want to attack me—
I pay God my thanks...

Psalm 57...

In Your wings I hide...
I call to God, the Most High
To awaken Dawn.

Psalm 58...

My tears flow in wrath,
At the evil wrought by man!
O God, reward good!

Psalm 59...

Enemies o'ercome!
Strength gone, O God, I plead—Come!
For You: make music!

Psalm 60...

I go down to depths...
Defeat is ours by Your hand...
O God, bring us help.

Psalm 61...

From earth's ends I call...
Lead me to the far, high rock
Where I sing to God.

Psalm 62...

God-rest for my soul...
In Him—my rock, my safety...
Strength belongs to God.

Psalm 63...

God, I pine for You...
My heart thirsts like dry, parched land...
Your hand supports me.

Psalm 64...

The evil-tongued fall...
God's protection is assured...
Proclaim God's power!

Psalm 65...

Praise and thanksgiving...
Our vows to God are fulfilled—
See, He gives richly.

Psalm 66...

Trial by fire is done...
Now's the time for thanksgiving.
Faithful love is God...

Psalm 67...

God blesses us so!
Earth has yielded its produce.
Let us revere God.

Psalm 68...

Yahweh! Heaven's Lord!
The gods of men's wars, no more!
Awesome Your power!

Psalm 69...

I endure disgrace;
O my Savior, answer me!
Your face Zion sees!

Psalm 70...

Yahweh, come help me!
Poor and needy as I am...
God, do not delay!

Psalm 71...

God, who is like You?
Now I am old and grey-haired...
I lift Your praise up.

Psalm 72...

O that the king come
With saving justice, O God!
To endure always...

Psalm 73...

They are swept away...
God, the wicked force destroy.
Yahweh, my refuge...

Psalm 74...

Did You reject me,
O God of blazing anger?
Do not forget us...

Psalm 75...

We give thanks to You...
Who comes to judge righteously.
In strength give God due.

Psalm 76...

All war'iors, heroes...
Silenced in terror and dread.
Acknowledge Yahweh.

Psalm 77…

When I am distressed
I ponder ancient glories…
And God's faithful love.

Psalm 78…

God so blessed and loved
His ever-straying people—
David was chosen.

Psalm 79…

We, Your chosen ones,
Suffer insult for our God.
Savior, please help us.

Psalm 80…

By Your hand it lived…
This sad vine—Your Israel.
God, return to us.

Psalm 81…

You cried out—I came!
But do not worship false gods…
I feed you pure wheat!

Psalm 82…

Justice for the weak!
The world's foundations totter…
O God, judge us all.

Psalm 83…

They would destroy You,
O Yahweh…stay not silent…
Let them seek Your Name.

Psalm 84…

Set on pilgrimage…
My whole being yearns and pines
For the courts of God.

Psalm 85…

You Who blot out sin…
Give us, my God, loyalty…
Peace and Justice kiss.

Psalm 86…

Listen to me, God…
For You do marvelous deeds…
Give unto me strength.

Psalm 87...

Zion: loved city—
Foundation on the mountain—
All will find home here...

Psalm 88...

Annihilated...
I can only now cry, "God"...
To the deep...in dark...

Psalm 89...

David—beloved,
God's promises eternal...
We suffer anger.

Psalm 90...

From eternity
You bring humans to the dust...
Let Your sweetness be.

Psalm 91...

Under wings—hidden!
No fear of terrors of night...
In Yahweh my life!

Psalm 92…

It is good to give
Thanks to God—music and joy!
The upright proclaim!

Psalm 93…

From eternity…
Yahweh rules majestic'ly.
The world is set firm.

Psalm 94…

Arise and shine forth!
Yahweh, please, I plead support…
Wicked overcome.

Psalm 95…

Harden not your hearts
As at Meribah/Massah…
Yahweh is our God.

Psalm 96…

Proclaim God's glory;
Tremble before Him, nations!
He judges justly.

Psalm 97...

Black cloud enfolds Him!
Ablaze, like wax mountains melt!
God is holiness!

Psalm 98...

To judge with justice...
The sea thunders—mountains shout!
Yahweh approaches!

Psalm 99...

Patriarchs—Your priests...
They obeyed the Law You gave.
Our God loves justice.

Psalm 100...

Serve Yahweh in song!
Thank Him! Acclaim His Great Name!
His love is faithful!

Psalm 101...

When You come to me...
O God, I walk blamelessly.
Evil I seek not...

Psalm 102...

God, I'm in trouble...
I (screech-owl) keep vigil—mo-o-an.
Lord of all, hear me!

Psalm 103...

Redeemed tenderly...
Bless Yahweh and His servants
Who love uprightly.

Psalm 104...

My God—great You are!
How countless Your works, Yahweh!
All my life I sing!

Psalm 105...

Sacred promise kept...
Israel from Egypt leapt...
Yahweh's chosen ones.

Psalm 106...

Horrendous evil—
Our history, our bleeding...
Save us, our Yahweh!

Psalm 107…

Whatever befalls…
Yahweh, ever faithful, sees—
Come to rescue me.

Psalm 108…

I will awake, Dawn…
God, bring us help in crisis…
You trample our foes.

Psalm 109…

Words brought me disgrace…
Those who were friends now find blame.
My God, help the poor.

Psalm 110…

Royal dignity…
A priest like Melchizedek…
He lifts his head high.

Psalm 111…

Deliverance sent…
Covenant lives forever…
Praise God and bless Him!

Psalm 112...

I delight in God—
And in fearing Him, am blessed...
The wicked are vexed.

Psalm 113...

Praise, servants of God!
From sun's rising to setting...
He lifts the needy.

Psalm 114...

Sea, what makes you flee?
Why skip like rams, you mountains?
God comes! Tremble earth!

Psalm 115...

The dead cannot praise—
Idol worship, man creates...
We living bless God!

Psalm 116...

My heart—be at peace...
Though brought low, I was rescued.
God, I call Your Name.

Psalm 117...

Praise God, all nations,
For His faithful love is strong!
His constancy is...

Psalm 118...

Give thanks to Yahweh...
His love endures forever...
Rock cornerstone strength.

Psalm 119...

Your Law is delight...
Beginning to end Your Word,
Yahweh, gives me life.

Psalm 120...

Yahweh answers me
When I call out in trouble.
Here people want war!

Psalm 121...

I lift up my eyes...
God neither sleeps nor slumbers...
and my life will guide.

Psalm 122...

The House of Yahweh,
Your Gates, O Jerusalem!
I pray for your peace!

Psalm 123...

Lord, I am in need...
From the heights in which You rule—
The jew'l of pity...

Psalm 124...

Israel escaped...
Because Yahweh blessed its name.
Our help is in Him.

Psalm 125...

Like Jerusalem...
Yahweh encircles His own.
Peace to Israel.

Psalm 126...

Zion's captives come;
Mouths filled with laughter and song...
Once weeping/no more.

Psalm 127...

Yahweh provides all.
His loved ones must toil and sweat
And trust Providence.

Psalm 128...

Fear Yahweh—be blessed!
Labor and walk in His ways
For prosperity...

Psalm 129...

All hating Zion—
The yoke of the wicked is
Shattered by Yahweh...

Psalm 130...

Listen to my pleas...
From the depths I cry to Thee!
Yahweh, faithful Love...

Psalm 131...

Like a little child
In mother's arms held silent...
I hope in Yahweh.

Psalm 132...

Remember David...
Who vowed to find a dwelling,
Yahweh's resting place...

Psalm 133...

Delightfully live
In love with one another...
See each as brother.

Psalm 134...

Through the night watches
Serving in the house of God...
May Yahweh bless you.

Psalm 135...

Make music—bring joy
In courts of God's holy house!
He dwells in Zion!

Psalm 136...

Yahweh is goodness
For His faithful love endures.
Give thanks to the Lord!

Psalm 137...

O Jerusalem!
I wept remembering you!
Where has my joy gone?

Psalm 138...

All my heart thanks You...
Though sublime and great is God—
The helpless have life...

Psalm 139...

Yahweh, You know me—
Knit me in my mother's womb...
Test me; guide my path.

Psalm 140...

Listen to me pray...
Yahweh, evil men attack.
Yet You give me life...

Psalm 141...

Yahweh, guard my mouth...
Unprotected, leave me not...
Save me from evil...

Psalm 142…

To Yahweh I cry…
I am miserably weak.
They persecute me.

Psalm 143…

Yahweh, I'm pleading…
A poor servant in trial—
Numb with fear, I hope…

Psalm 144…

Yahweh, blessed rock!
Prepares for battles/shields us…
And fills every need.

Psalm 145…

I praise God, my King!
Tenderness, pity, and love…
Bless forevermore!

Psalm 146…

Praise Yahweh, my soul!
Put no trust in humankind…
Only God can save!

Psalm 147…

Praise Yahweh—sing psalms—
Who gathers the exiles home—
Filled with finest wheat.

Psalm 148…

Praise God—all heavens!
Angelic heights—praise His Name!
Praise Sublimity!

Psalm 149…

Israel rejoice!
Sing a new song to Yahweh!
Nations' judgment passed!

Psalm 150…

Praise Almighty God!
Praise with dance/song/instruments!
Praise with all your breath!

Part II

Meditations for the Occasions of Your Life

A Wedding

When God's Divine Love is shared in this most sacred
bonding...
A tenderness beyond compare—God grants to us in precious
founding—
Here on earth a taste of heaven above. This special and unique
love shows
How much God intimately wants us learning to know and grow
For Him. So renew your hearts in Him prayerfully each moment
day by day.
Join in Him together—in body, mind, and soul. Give this way
To your family to hold in security and strength—so they not stray
From Christ's Body—we are keeping you in our prayers. We say,
"Let not earthly trials hold you—be close from their weight...
O Lord, shower blessings on this wedding, and ever reign
Sovereign in their hearts. Come Holy Spirit without delay!
These vows of union with Thee in Love's eternity to sway."

A Birth of a Baby

As once was born in Bethlehem a child so warm and fair…
Is born to you a little one for whom you now must care.
We hope to give you courage in your journey with this birth.
We will walk and talk and help you with any questions here on Earth.
Your parish fam'ly prays and tends you here while you walk with God.
Can you imagine any better or by whom else you've been so awed?
God's love is needed by each person—it is never hindered, never stopped!
So bask in peace, and joy, and loving—these are always oh, so close
When babies come because the dear Lord always knows
How necessary that these are to us—so that you can love bestow…

On Illness

Suffering is never easy, never a delight; not what we want, and yet...
Jesus said, "Take up your cross and follow me!" We wonder why,
When misery is all that we can see. Lord, give me the vision; the set
Of eyes and ears to perceive, too, "My yoke is easy, my burden light."
Because somewhere in here—where goodness and evil meet—is HE
Who wants only the best for me. Help me to trust, my Savior;
To look for the Light in the darkness! Please turn any wavering
Into strength—for the whole of my life's length... And burn away
My doubt in the fires of Your Divine Love so I can surely gain
The gates of Heaven and see Your Face when comes my eternal day...
For it is not the cross You and I've borne that will endure
But the Love worn patiently under it—heaven will ensure!

On the Loss of a Child

When the searing loss of my child, my own, occurs, I moan
In utter anguish and grief. And yet I know this loss was hers—
Dear Mother Mary—who holds my heart in hope of peace. Groan
To God though I do—the prophets, too, allow. How the lure
Of the Sorrows the Blessed Mother endured fill me with love
And compassion for fellow humankind, who suffered through
Similar disasters. Jesus, You Who gave Your Body and Blood
So that we may have Life Eternal, we give You Your due...
I turn my agony to high hymns of praise to Almighty You...
Reaching into places of courage I knew not I have. You are
Truth—
And I seek You; You are Beauty—and I behold in this sad world You
Holding out that which is also You—Love—to me in the good
People praying and weeping with me... O, Lord imbue
My tears with healing...in You and through You... Amen...

On the Loss of a Spouse

On my beloved, My Lord, I seek Your eternal rest and peace...
May the heavens open and grant my spouse all that will not
cease...
Eternally-given joy, filled-to-full love and abundance—given ALL
That You are—ALL that You have promised... Savior, Your call
For my own is what I here seek. Listen also to the prayers of these
Others, who companion me, and whose prayers peak to Thee...
You know I haven't asked for me, dear God, for I am meek
But need You, oh so much right now, for fear and grief are seeds
That sow my heart quite ceaselessly. So I can trust You
endlessly—
Fill my aching soul with knowledge of Your Divine Love—the key
To my hope of Eternal Life and Resurrection in You—so I'm free
To be all I know You want me to be—lover of You, Holy Trinity.

Baptism of a Baby

Bubbling Waters of Eternal Life call forth new hope, new life…
And you, dear parents, are called forth to lead and to guide
This young child into the faith that is yours—and this is truly gift
Which Christ gives us—the gift of Christ's Church. We lift
Our hearts with those of your family today and forever
As you enter into this most marvelous endeavor…
We are now with you by our most precious prayers…
We will walk with you—and be with you—as time goes by.
Just ask for help anytime; we are willing to try…
This massive village is there for your support. And, do not deny,
God, Himself, is there for you, He's the Ultimate Abide…
So PEACE, JOY, AND WONDER with this little one
As Divine Love overflows from God's own loving Son…

After the Easter Vigil—for the Neophytes

These life-giving waters are the very key to what you are...
Adopted "son" of the Father Creator in Jesus' Holy Name.
Therefore, you have keys to divinity—although we wander far...
These waters free you from all that you have done—but fame
And fortune seek you, too—so freedom means little, often,
Through prayer, study, and the support of us—those who listen
Well-learn true riches and peace-of-mind. We, loving be,
Belong to the One Who Is Yet Three, and gloriously
We come to love like Him Whom we come to seek.
When we've met Him in Eucharist and in Confirmation see
The Trinity and We in Holy Unity gifted as we are
Compared to these. But God gives this generously to thee...
—we truly begin "to be"...

Confirmation—for Adults

A journey begun was not yet complete without you,
O Holy Mother Church. You nourished me with teachings
That led me to true inner freedom; and then, what few
Would proclaim or understand—with the Holy Spirit preaching
That freedom was then absorbed in my soul… Can you know
What utter joy you bring to me in this long yearning searching
For which I've walked many a mile? Though I struggle so
With some of those mysterious meanings—I admit, I am blind
To my own faults and wrong-leanings; you accept me although
I am human and weak. I rely too much on my wayfaring mind.
For my gracious and glorious God I will be humble and meek.
Holy Spirit, grant me Divine Love, this is what I seek. Amen.

Confirmation—for Children

As the bishop said, "Be sealed with the Holy Spirit,"
And with the sacred oil anointed my forehead...
My eyes were opened and I saw those things (quiet, quiet)
I had never seen quite the same way before—led
By my holy guardian angel—my soul knew God
Better than it did before. The Holy Spirit's gifts
Are treasures I seek and by which I am always awed;
I praise the Holy Trinity to Whom I lift
My child's voice in loving thankfulness;
And to Jesus, especially, Whom I know best...

The Tenth Anniversary of a Priestly Ordination

Dear Father, you chose to shepherd Christ's people—a flock
You would lead as you fight all His battles. The door that you knocked
These ten years ago—is the door to the heart of your own
Shepherd King.
No doubt, you had no idea right away He would your own
heartstrings ring...
And peril and God's law is your lot as His anthems you sing. What
joy you bring
To the Word when you preach the Truth—you uphold ALL HE IS
In whatever you do... And because the Sacrifice Eternal is never
finished...
Our love for you, Father, will never be diminished...
But quietly and beneath the divinity involved, humanity here
speaks, too...
We thank you, Father, for being you.

Loss of a Parent

Now, O Lord, with the loss of this, my dear parent,
I come to you in grief. Yes, but with the added pain
Of my own mortality that is so apparent
Now it seems. I turn to You in anguish with hope to gain
The strength I need. I am aware that I am not where
You would have me be spiritually because You care—
And want me to be free to let loose of woe and misery
To be held in Your strong hands—the agony spare...
And with You share the crosses and my destiny...
So that peace can overflow my heart and I can wear
The badge of eternity You give to me in abundance...
Savior, to You...
            in remembrance...

First Eucharist

Jesus, is that You, the substance of the bread?
You are so white, so little, and so very plain...
Could it be You to Whom I bow my head?
I know You once were a little child the same
As me—your littleness is clear and real...
But I know when I eat You, Precious Host—love
For You, dear Jesus, and my friends I'll feel
Stirred right up. Wine in cup—it's Your Blood!
I taste gifts for me! It's for me—especially:
To let me eat finest wheat! Drink to make me holy—
Like You! To be connected with all in Your Peace!

Seventy-Fifth Birthday

Three-quarters of a century in which I have been
Living, working, striving to be a good person. Faith
Has carried me through those tough times—and win
A few, lose a few—I've learned on my Lord to gaze...
Because only when I'm true with Him does life make
Total sense. Well, mostly anyway—there's those things
About which we only guess—for heaven's sake—
And they don't contentment bring...so let Truth loudly ring!
I'll sing my praises of my Lord, my Savior King
On this my day of celebration! And don't forget to mention
What wondrous gifts of God's blessing—our lives,
And all the abundance in them to us God surprises!

On the Ordination of a Deacon

Called to proclaim the Gospel and to acts of charity...
You are blessed with sacred holiness proper to deacons,
And in this we give you our most profound thanks—as freely
Given as you have offered your call to us. A beacon
Of light it is—seen by those of us who suffer in misery
And darkness—to whom you've reached out in compassion
And agape, divine love... And we will share our stories
With you—in exchange for the Sacred Gospel, the lasting
Peace of God, you will sing songs to us. Then the glory!
O brother mine, bring us the Word so we won't be blind...

Graduation from College

A certain temerity grips the heart of a dear college graduate
Upon thinking of embarking on life's responsibilities...
One likes to think one is perfectly self-reliant...
And immortal, self-possessed, and full of abilities.
But honestly speaking looking out on the mess that is left
Of the world by the older generations one wonders why
They didn't see all the answers so clear to oneself...
Best not said at all—God intends here wisdom to not deny...
Providence—not oneself—provides for the universe...
I can make a big difference, but I am not God.
Wide though the difference between Him and me—
I have my part to play—and I will, if He will me fill.
Between God and me—we'll fit the bill!

Fiftieth Wedding Anniversary

Cherish me forever, my precious one, my own;
These words of love—those vows to God we've said—
My, how they've been tested! What seeds time's sown!
Could we have ever guessed back when we were wed
What blessings would come from just being old—
And seeing what the fruits of our labors have meant...
Or what we simply and quite innocently told
Our children—and where these were built and sent!
No matter what has happened, we together grow
Beyond and above it. Eternity draws us so
Tightly that God holds us here below
In a band of gold...

Priestly Ordination

With the laying on of hands, you, my brother, become Father.
And like to Christ, His Priestly duties are now yours for life
And for the betterment of His people. The Blessed Mother,
Your earthly Queen and Protectress sends her soft sighs
Heavenward as you lay prostrate before the marble altar…
Before God and humankind; signifying the humility
With which you will clothe yourself with the priestly collar—
Adornment to be worn with spiritual simplicity—
No matter the abundance of grace with which God grants you…
And to whom is given the peace, fulfillment, and joy of a few…
For it is the cross which we seek and endue…
And Jesus Christ we must transfuse…

Religious Vows

O holy vows of modesty and strength; royal vestments that infuse
Jesus Christ into my mind, heart, and soul...as I profess those words
With courage—for what the future bears I know not because I lose
All sight of it for Him Who Is Everything... The sacred bonding burns
Into my soul with its flame of Holy Spirit—the dross flies lightly by—
Caught on the updraft of my purification, accomplishes so handily
While God and the angels stand and watch my tears and smile deny
My passivity... Union with Him; union with a community...
An eternal life of thankfulness and giving-ness to Almighty
Thee...

When Fear Is About to Overcome

As fear sets its sights on my soul, I remember Jesus in the boat—
Asleep in the storm. He is my model, my strength in this life...
As I remember, His friends were afraid, the evangelist wrote—
They awoke Him in terror. Does that sound familiar? What strife
We find to take to Him so... And what were His words? "You
Who have so little faith...why are you so frightened?" Although
Some would say these words sound more like a kind of rebuke—
We know they are truth... We little ones lack courage; woe
To us who do not place our trust in Him who holds us strongly
In His arms. For He says again and again, "Fear not!" "I am
With you always—even unto the end of the world." Eternally
Existing with the Creator is Divine Love through the Sacrificial
Lamb.

When Faced with Death

The moment hits us with the stark suddenness and reality
Of an ice-cold wave of water; our breath is dashed away—
Or perhaps we feel numb, uncertain, and far removed: actually
Not of this life at all... The cost of shock—the body's escape
From pain was not unknown to Jesus, either. Yet He, in agony,
Reached into that place of Divine Love and gave and gave
To us so that we may be free to do the same—and give ourselves
To the self-same Light we must keep before our faces to gain
Both ourselves and the world. So we must remember to delve,
No matter what the apparent cost to us, into our inner strength
To save our souls—and whomever we can take with us—for Home
In Paradise where wide open are awaiting the shining golden gates.
Remember you will never want again—you will never again be alone.
This is the moment of your life for which you have always waited...

On Graduation from High School

Your mother and father have held their breath waiting for this:
Could you, would you be able to compete well enough to finish?
Somewhere in you there is a big heart that wanted and worked...
And you knew that inside you a certain Someone lurked...
Who gives you courage and strength to keep on going when it hurts...
Someone that some kids don't have (at least they don't admit it!)
Who's a friend for life—but about whom many would keep quiet!
Would you dare to speak of Him to all who ask you? Or is the cost
Too high in college life? Don't let your values be forgotten or lost
In the mainstream... Jesus Christ is the name written on your heart.
His thrilling story of Divine Love will give your life a real jump-start.
You are a winner because you already know the story of the glory!

On the Spiritual Loss of a Loved One

Be it child, brother, sister, cousin; the lost one gone away
From our hearts—far from the nest—to a place of danger
And perhaps of unrest... We see so clearly the stay
Of the journey in pieces and disquiet... Yet Mary, no stranger
To loss of a loved one, left Jesus—yet a young boy,
In the crowds of Jerusalem. And do you remember
Where she found Him? Yes, in the temple regaled—no toy—
By the priests and the rabbis—and teaching them
Was He... Do you think you, too, can take a lesson
From dear Mary and Jesus? Think hard here, you must...
And leave the rest in His hands, which are strong. Run
Not away—go straight to Him who has mercy and is just...
For He will listen and answer your prayers for this lost one.

On Being Tempted

After Jesus was baptized He went straight into the desert and prayed...
And there He was tempted by Satan in His weakness having fasted
Forty days... Satan tested Jesus on things that must have left Him
amazed...
To give Jesus the hardest tests Satan could imagine—he handily
crafted.
Do you sometimes feel that way yourself? Do you feel "up against it"?
Try as much as you might—you cannot avoid the seducer's wiles
In the midst of the night? "I am not Jesus," you say, "but lest it
Overpower me, I can only run as fast as I can for many a mile."
And in this God will bless you—for you will not give it sway here.
Then you can even run to the doors of the Church near your home...
For Jesus is knocking at the doors of your heart—He's there
To sustain you where-ever you roam... No matter where you're going
Or what you're doing He is right within you—and ALWAYS cares.
"Ask and you shall receive; seek and you shall find..."
And do you know what? Jesus was even found by the blind...

On the Fortieth Anniversary of a Priestly Ordination

The shepherd of an earthly flock who leads so tenderly
We see where he, too, sees the need to suffer like Christ—
So very passionately for us. As Christ, in person, he
Tends the Sacrifice Eternal giv'n our souls to best entice
Toward Paradise—how perfectly we see it done! O God,
Our friend, this priest You've called, is more to us than gold.
His talents and his kindness make him a giant—we are simply awed.
So be present to him, dear Savior; keep him in the fold...
We want him as our pastor forever—until he's grown too old...
Then there's home for him in Heaven 'cause he fits the mold.

After the Sacrament of Penance

O Dear and Loving Savior of My Own, Jesus Christ,
You, Who abandoned Your identity to be like me, a sinner—
Have wiped my slate clean by Your mercy—white like
The milk that feeds an infant. I shall be that winner
That feeds upon Thee in the Eucharist that also completes
And heals me—Your child waiting for You in Your Glory
To come finish this magnificent plan of Yours. I bleed
Tears of pain, yes; but also joy knowing Your story.
The best is yet to come! Alleluia's my life's creed!

Upon Losing Patience with Another

We are so self-preoccupied...so concerned with that of
ourselves...
(It is "me, me, ME" and I cry out loudly to THEE!)
Someone else intrudes on our self-space—into our thought-space—
And we lash out with impatience...now we know we don't feel well.
We are bothered, guilty, and remorseful...all is terrible waste...
We see the eyes of our brethren, who did nothing at all
deserving...
We are hounded by this—but push it back into our subconscious.
Why do we go on like this? Why don't we ever seem to begin learning
From our bad feelings? Our tempers go unchecked into the
future. Lost
Is any help for us because we "forget" our lessons from God... Yet
There IS help in the form of others who can help us grow—to seek
This help is God-fearing and God-loving... So set
Your eyes upon God—learn His ways so He will bless you
abundantly...

Substituting "Idols" for God

God created our souls with a big, empty, black kind of hole...
That we insist on filling up with all sorts of "idols" except God...
But only God fills that hole because it's so big... Look below
Or above, around or within. You won't find anything that awes
Quite like God—no matter how hard you try (and people do!)
People even try to fill up with themselves—how silly this is!
Nothing will even come close, except God; how about you?
Perhaps you have tried power, money, sex, drugs, or even kids...
People will try anything it's so compelling—or they're blue...
But just try God—He's the answer, you know. Only This
Will be just right to fill that big, empty hole inside of you...

A Meditation on the Blessed Virgin Mary

Do you know the significance of always being available
To God Almighty—throughout your whole life—no matter what?
That is the most meaningful pronouncement (incredible
Isn't it?) of "perpetual virginity" I ever heard... No such
Idea or thought could be inspired by human alone—the Holy Spirit,
Divine Love, teaches us Truth in the splendor of Light...
And without Christ she'd be nothing...like us, could not finish
A sentence even—and it would be dark as the night...
But she said, Yes, in obedience, love, and freewill—
And the Day-Sun sprang forth for her and us to fill
So that sin and the grave would never again kill...
And all nations will learn to call her blessed "for real"
And generations of people will peace instill...
As they look to her eyes turned to Christ on the hill.

A Bedtime Blessing

The day has ended, and I'm tired, dear Lord. Grant me
A night without dreary dreams—sleep with simple peace...
As I look back upon my waking hours I can only see
That I have erred aplenty—but, My Loving Friend, least
That I am, I have tried to be faithful to You. Please be
Patient as I stumble through the paths so rocky they cease
Being visible to the naked eye—Your Eyes are needed
To negotiate this journey—for Your help I humbly plead...
But thank you, Savior, for all of it; forgive me for the seeds
Of sin, and for the sins I've most horrifically completed...
I am helpless—for without You I am nothing and oh, so weak...
But for now quiet my mind and let me bask in Your rest...
In deepest silence I would be most comfortably blessed.
You have remained to me the most loyal and the truest...
So to You I'll cleave securely—so sleep will come renewing....

A Mealtime Blessing

Your abundance and nourishment we always seek while we sow
Your friendship and fellowship with this meal while we grow...
Into Your image and likeness with each bite, every sip, every word.
Likewise, making home Heaven where You'll be adored...
Let cheer, love, peace, and friendship abound—on the table
Here and abroad... So God's Kingdom is found—not a fable,
But in Truth all around. Hallelujah! Jesus is Lord! Let the song ring
From the ceiling down to the floor! Let us sing! Let us sing!

On Doubt

Just think of doubt as a gateway…to a bigger, purer faith;
Jesus didn't send St. Thomas away—nor did He foster guilt…
And He will forgive you yours—if you confess to Him today.
Bring your doubt to Light—and with Knowledge your mind fill.
For Truth is near when prayer becomes your constant friend…
When surrender and trust become radical—doubt becomes His Will
And part of the lifetime journey on which He has you sent…
To the center of His Gracious and Immaculate Heart which bleeds
For love of you. So you see, doubt is where you and He meet—
Deep in that darkness you greet…

When You Feel Abandoned

There comes that time of abject agony—when all seems lost...
And there is nowhere to turn; even God seems to have turned away...
I am in utter blackness—everything dear to me is not worth the cost...
My faith, a lifetime of abundance, has left me dry—no stay
In this time of trouble... Then I remember the words of Christ,
"My God, my God, why have You abandoned me!" He cried!
My own personal agonies—so near, dear, and hurting—are wiped
Free of injury and are now turned outward! So hear the wide
Expanse of my pride and know that others, too, suffer this!
Say I! Even Christ, Himself, tender with the Love of God, knew
Pain of abandonment! So ordinary I could not help but list
Under such duress! Thank you for this insight that renews
My faith in You—O Holiness! Although I'm not yet through with
You...

On Forgiveness

There are those times when forgiveness seems impossible...
When you just can't let someone "off the hook," or say
A kind word for them down in your heart... There is no lull
For your soul in this—it is engrained and you know it stains.
Let yourself know, dearest one: this is not about "them"...
This is your journey in coming to know the fullness of mercy
That is YOURS from the Lord—from His LOVE, where it stems...
This love is boundless and deep—and is completely "simplicity."
The cost doesn't count when you give it back endlessly...
Because "my yoke is easy; my burden is light." So peacefully
And joyfully submit in fullness to this bountiful harmony.

In the Quiet Times

These moments of peaceful quiet are rare, indeed, my Savior...
My life so hurriedly is passing me by—I cannot think or breathe.
So now I turn to You for gift of contemplation—I'm braver
To ask than before—but these moments I now must seize...
Your rest is where I long to be—so, Dear One, unclutter mind
Of all it holds and empty me...so with You I can fill completely.
You know I cannot, of myself, do anything...for I am blind,
Deaf, and handicapped but for Your Will. So be with me—
In fact—unite with me so that I know You as You Are—
Oh, that my desires be Your Will! That I never be from You far!

When an Answer to a Prayer Isn't Forthcoming

O Gifter of All Gifts and Mercies, You know that I have asked
Endlessly for a particular favor…but there has been no answer.
Why is this, Lord? What is so difficult? Why haven't I been blessed?
You, Who can do anything can do this for me. I've learned
To bring EVERYTHING to You! So what is this heartlessness?
Could the answer be "no"? Do you think I'm ready to hear this—
O Most High One? Is that why You are silent to my prayers?
Yesterday my friend asked me just where my prayers would finish—
And I confess that I do not know the final consequences—where
These prayers would lead…I'm beginning to see differently now,
Because You've led me down another road…Jesus, allow
Me the grace to say, "I'm sorry for not trusting You." I bow
To Your Almighty Power and trust in You forever…

On Freedom

So you want freedom…for what? to crash and burn?
    to mope and yearn?
        to complete some harm?
           to fearfully die alone?
…and what's your goal?
    For the Lord knows…

We are not masters of ourselves—this deception grows…
And the seeds it sows bring death to our souls.
If joy and hope you would have, Christ is the saving salve…
To our wounds of despair and pride; no—there's no need even to hide…
For we are community—and we all have sins others can see,
But we love eternally because Jesus lives centrally.
He is our Authority—and with this can we be free.
To learn to choose to live life abundantly
        with love, grace, and dignity.

On the Death of a Loved One

Dear, sweet Providence:
You, Who care for the birds and the bees,
    ...for the flowers, the trees, and me...
I give unto THEE...
My ALL to Your Abundance and Riches
    ...to You Who bless us
With unbridled magnificence...
Because I know we will forever be
    part of THEE
When You are ALL-IN-ALL
    (and how You enthrall!)

Upon Adoration of the Blessed Sacrament

Tabernacle holy in which You reside, my Sacred Love,
    Make so my body; make so my blood...
That the Mass in which was the consecration...
    For the most ordinary becomes Divine contemplation
So each can experience this abundant adoration
    Which brings me closer, closer to You 'til union—
Like to Eucharist itself—that Christ fusion
    Locks Substance to substance and Mind to mind;
...yes, we were blind...
But now we see—
And You're the Key...
One-Yet-Three.

In Spiritual Trials

When being overcome with trial—when feeling undone…
When wanting to complain with pain, and wanting to run…
Anxiety rules my head—distraction or dryness reigns o'er my prayer.
I've turned to Jesus, asked for forgiveness—it seems He's not there.
Where are You, my God? You, Who promised me…
That if I knocked, the door would open; if I asked, I'd receive…
When I look, I then know…humbly seeing this, too, is gift—
My whole being to You—Who are not satisfied with
Mediocrity—but wants my best. So I give it all with love—
Though it means MY body and MY blood,
Sacrificing my very honor and pride,
Which are nothing but weights inside…
The glory is in "nothing to You denied…"

When We Offend the One We Love the Most

This ominous story of our own grievous fall in humanity…
Humanity could be so glorious—if we'd only be "true to it."
We try to "run and hide" or betray a real simplicity
By cover-ups and worse, a terrible blow—duplicity… Yet,
To do God's will requires an easy "yes." For a fee,
And a high one, we avoid it surreptitiously.
Surrendering is easier—it yields warmth, and truth,
And freedom—and realizing God's gifts are free
To those who want not mediocrity… But He
Who is Giver of LIFE ETERNALLY-FOUND
And eternally-lived by those heaven-bound,
Leads us surely there…with nary a single sound.

On Perfectionism

"So be perfect," said our Lord Jesus, speaking to the people…
"Just as your heavenly Father is perfect," He declared.
Do you have thoughts on how this could even be reasonable?
Or are you one who holds yourself to this rule? Have you fared
Well; or are you subject to righteousness, pride,
And judgmental-ism like so many of us? We seek
Blindly, don't we? The "perfection" must be "love that is wide"…
This giving love can only come from a heart that is meek—
Or we can't receive the imperfect gifts humans give in
"compassion"
To us out of their own imperfect love—like ours… Our passion
For perfection drives us to unreason and disquiet; lasting
Peace and joy is not ours to have and hold. Surrender this, too…
For if God's mercy and abundance you want to see… You
Thank the Lord for your gifts—and "offer up" a sacrifice of a few
Flaws of your own, lovingly, lovingly, laughing as you do…

When Life Seems Overwhelming

When our lives seem too much…
When the world seems lost and unmanageable…
When the mission God gives us seems impossible—for we are
   too little
To make an impact… It seems God has us right where He wants us—
   …meek and redeemable…
These "hidden" ways of God come to light
   to show Him to be quite reasonable.
It's only we who are blind—
   and these plans we don't always understand…
   (nor do we need to know…)
When we have faith to grow
   into a binding trust
That gives us what we must
Have in order to have peace
That lasts eternally…
Then I'm free deep in the heart of me.

When God Seems to Ask Too Much of Me

Oh, my load seems so much; my burden is so heavy!
O Lord, are You really asking this much of me?
I'm not really certain I can bear up under this much longer—
Do I pray to be made to endure more—to be made stronger?
Peace be unto you—O little one of God! You are meek—
And have believed—and have borne the cross most patiently…
There are those grand plans to which we are not privy—
For we are mortal humankind…but rest assured,
There are others who know your plight—and are forewarned—
Whose prayers and actions will help make it right…
Eventually, somewhere: yes, even in heaven itself
Where all the saints in front of God have knelt
Praying and interceding for you and others of your ilk.
These prayers work miracles, and for you are spilt!

When Contentment Is Beyond My Grasp

I've looked through philosophies…
    Tried most theologies…
        Owned most everything…
            Yet here remains this restlessness
And I long for strength and real inner peace…
Humanity and its trappings fail me.
Where do I seek?
Have you ever looked "inside"—opened yourself to "contemplate"?
Empty yourself of all that is "you"—simply wait…
Until you find that certain inward filling
(Here it helps to be desirous and willing)
Some call "God"
And feel "spell-bound" and "highly-awed"…
For there is nothing to compare—
And this usually translates to "everywhere"…
but particularly you'll meet this in silence…
    deep in your soul-center you'll greet this…
        and then you'll desire to mine this…
as treasure beyond measure…
Thus satisfied, joy overflows to pure bliss…
Then theology's Mysteries come to completeness.
And best of all—it's pure "gift."

On the Fiftieth Birthday

I've spent my life in work one way or another; so today
I look back on those times, realizing what lies ahead
Is going to take much, much more than what was then: faith...
Faith that I'll get through, with God's help, where I'm led—
Going fearlessly (or so I would hope) into an unknown future
Not knowing how to cope, except for my Jesus friend,
Who loves me more than I ever could begin to feature...
So as I begin to take account of this life I have lived—
I foresee the opportunities in front of me to spread...
Love all around like a fountain—like it's been given
To me in abundance (and what a God to Whom I'm driven!)

When Feeling Unworthy of God's Love

My God, You know by my tainted nature, I am not
Worthy to receive the Body and Blood of Your Son—
Yet You deigned to come down from heaven; caught
In a fleshly body and tortured to death—You won
For us freedom from sin and death...while we were yet
Sinful and corrupt. So, dear Savior, this in itself shows
Us the essential goodness of our creation and what
Love that You have for us in our lawlessness... Know
Me, O Blest Creator, as agonized over sinfulness and heal
This wretchedness. For You Who Love us though incomplete
Will fulfill holiness in us though Christ Who Redeems. Amen.

Why Go to Mass Every Day?

Have you ever been so in love with someone you couldn't
Get that one out of your thoughts? Well, it could be
That beautiful with God, too (if you let it...) God wouldn't
Stop a process like that from becoming, if you could see
It this way... It's like participating in God's very own
Being—an awe-striking glimpse into heaven which we
Can only begin to understand when we have grown
In our knowledge and trust in God. This is fostered
In the Sacrifice Eternal in unity with the Body of Christ
As our neighbors. It is time to put aside all that is bothered—
Unite with the Body of Christ in Eucharist...
This Sacred Mystery awaits all in Divine Love—the Passion
Of Jesus is ours, too, in each of our daily lives in one way or
fashion.

On Spiritual Simplicity

A word of modern derision has become near foolishness…
"Simplicity"—in all its plain-ness—truly has strength
Because it's yes, yes to God. In this we are blessed—
Like the Virgin Mary, the most simple one of all. The length
Of her life she said, "yes." No matter what befell—prophecy
Most terrible, exile, loss of child, torture and death of son—
These and more she endured for love of God her King!
And we, my friend, are called to this, too. Simplicity is won…
When we do\ love that loyally\ we are free humanity!

Meditation on "I Believe"

"I believe…" these words under which I stand—to which I belong
Mean much more than "a conclusion open to dispute."
These are not "opinion," which implies that I could be wrong…
No! It's absolute goodness, here, that follows suit.
"I believe" means "Jesus is Lord!"—the living creed,
And whether or not you, personally, believe…
He died for you and the unbelieving world as well.
This "Daddy" Existing in Glory came down among us to dwell
And to live this human life, tortured and agonized as in hell
Himself…took our flawed and sinful characters to His Precious
Soul…
And made us whole as He arose from death giving life eternal
By His Body and Blood with His Love… How can we give Him
any less
Than "I believe" in ALL THAT HE IS; in ALL THAT HE GIFTS!"

Meditation on the Passion

Life often leaves us little time to ponder, think, and conceive;
Much less do we allow ourselves room to fantasize and dream...
Our loss is palpable and in it we are not free.
But an important point is that Jesus' death is for you and me—
And the story of it is unparalleled and gives us depth
In our journey...so consider it carefully, even daily;
The riches are unfathomable. You will find God blesses
You with such success in heavenly knowledge
That our lives, which seem that of a massive ordeal,
Are in His bleeding and pierced Heart tenderly concealed...
Then He will wipe the cross's lingering traces
From your soul as it soars
in the heat of Love's fiery blazes...
And you will find rest and peace in heaven's ecstasies.

Am I an Easter Person?

As Christians we're called to be Easter people; to hold Christ in our hearts…
To proclaim Him "risen," to others given—our energy in Love Divine…
So how're we doin'? Is He risen in our hearts of flesh? Or are we apart—
And are our hearts really "made of stone"? So set your line…
For the fishin's good! There's work to do a'plenty. Because we love the Lord—
He made us hale and hearty to make HIM worshipped and adored!

On God's Gifts

In our ordinary lives, and ordinary being it is so easy...
To forget to see—all around us the beauty, the bounty,
Even within the very poverty...that is "me."
The gratitude which I know I forget to feel
Is gift, too...for without it I am bitter and weak.
O, dear Savior, within this very foolishness
I desire to please...
And to feel fully the love You have for me...
For otherwise I am purposeless and lonely.
All goodness is in You—Gifter of Eternity...
Extend upon me the ability to truly BE
ONE WITH THEE, ONE-YET-THREE!

Love Myself?

Jesus said, "Love your neighbor as yourself." And this
Most elemental rule tells much about you...
For it says to love yourself, does it not? Quick
Now, your response? "How can I be humble, too?"
Perhaps you've heard, "Blessed are the poor in spirit,"
And wondered what THAT meant... It's when we
Empty ourselves of us—and fill with God—that we merit
Happiness. Babies are "full of themselves"—see
Them grow aware of others... We, too, develop
Most completely as we learn this lesson of "poverty."
For we can only love ourselves fully, humbly, and truthfully,
When we see with God's eyes faithfully.

On Surrender

You may have heard the word "surrender" our friends
In Islam use—and know that Christians use it, too…
It doesn't mean "beat a hasty retreat" or any sense
That attack occurred…but that something spiritually due
Is being rendered to…and even more to the point—
Yielding or "letting go." (Just what would one "let go?"
And more important—to whom?) In the desire to join
Our hearts, minds, and lives to God we do so…
(What?)…surrender. We seek God in all ways known
To us—both out of righteousness, but mostly out of love…
Jesus taught us that God is "Daddy"—even though we're grown…
Surrendering to "Daddy" all our weaknesses, our will, and such,
Make us much more human. Only in God can we seek
The very peak of our humanity—the lesson that surrendering in
love teaches…
Surrendering EVERYTHING to God-On-High;
For us the height of heaven reaches.

On "Stumbling Blocks"

There are those questions and concerns which become
So troublesome they cannot be ignored…
They begin to confound our faith or some
May even cause doubt and dismay. Or perhaps we store
Them up—for a big burst of disbelief. Why not
Be aware—and bring them to a priest? Like the whole
Question of "Did God create evil?" Here we are caught
Between not fully explainable Mystery and human souls—
Who want "to know." And we who believe that "all
Is purposeful" trust this, too, has meaning. So
Seek that Truth through prayer and learning; but recall
That God is the Master Builder and the Sole Author
Whose Grand Plan's revealing comes when He allows.

On "Tolerance"

We who know the richness and abundance of our faith
Feel deep sadness when confronted by unbelief...
And some in the faith who know Christ as "the way,
The truth, and the life" can only know and see
Christianity like theirs as the righteous path to God—never mind
That Jews and Muslims serve the same God—or Buddhists
Pray to "the unknowable." Who, here, is really blind?
Jesus, Himself, on the cross had His Divine Identity tested
And removed from consciousness; "My God, why
Have You abandoned me?" Our own deep faith could be
Tested to the limit—by God in His Great Eternity... My!
This human poverty of ours is in the hands of God...
Let us drink deeply of it—and by our neighbors be awed!
For the One Who gives us our identities and faiths
Has declared that by loving each other we give Him laud...
We are "human poverty"—and this, this is Christ's way.

On Security

We who have so much to share often do not care
From whence comes our help, our strength, our lives—
We feel so satisfied... But deep inside we wear
Our insecurity—and for our future we strive...
To build up "equity", funds, pensions, and such
Beyond our simple need. God and the Church call
This "sin"—it is simply "greed." If we "need" too much
It seems that all might be taken away. We now all
Are hearing that money might lose value and meaning...
Is this God "writing on the wall"?
See this not as punishment—but as loving; it's seeming
To push us "where we want not to go..." to each other—
With all our foibles; to Jesus, our Redeemer and Brother—
Who did the Father show. And Mary, the Mother,
Protectress, and Queen of Martyrs, leads us in wonder.
While we marvelously grow nearer to Splendor,
Holy Spirit—so our love perfectly bestows...

The Cross Is Not Folly

On this day: The Exultation of the Cross, I wish to gift
Fellow Christians' understandings with how to lift
What to others seems simply silly—how Jesus died—
And why in a few short words… So our lives—
Filled with evil and sins (which you can't deny
Because no matter how hard you try they're there
Before your eyes)—can be made like God's (yes, where
We were once mortal humankind—we can be divinized!)
By Jesus' Passion on that throne of wood—in utter love
He gave up His connection as Son of God with blood
And in agony—not to worship His own Kingship or glory—
But to honor the poverty of us and our own stories
And turn the worst violence and hatred to Divine Love.
This is what we are asked to do with our body and blood…
Could I do this, Lord?—only You know if I would…

On Watching and Waiting

In Christianity we are always watching and waiting...
Which for some looks far too distant or fills them with impatience
Instead of joy of expectancy and pitch of fervor to get it all done
Before Christ's arrival in glory...yet, it really is fun
To realize the Kingdom is here already—filling our hearts with
the story
Of the essential meaning of existence—and the port of our moorings!
But to know goodness is triumphant no matter what
Evil befalls us—shows us God's way is the ultimate Just
Way, so we can give up our righteousness (from its source—
Which is "pride" and our ever-present downfall, of course.)
So let's "watch and wait" together...to the sublime future of us all...
When we're together as ONE with God—and LOVE is our only
recall.

Part III

Prayer-Poems written in the year 2006-2007
on the theme of mainly love-psalms
and those to be shared with others.

February 12, 2006
Sixth Sunday in Ordinary Time

On pondering "courage" after giving that advice to my
brother...on thinking of that virtue so lacking in our country
today in the face of a concocted "terrorism"...on thinking of
FDR and his famous quote, "The only thing we have to fear is fear
itself."

Even psalmists give the cogent words, "take courage,
Be stouthearted, wait for the Lord." How can we free
Persons—proud and strong—cower; giving homage
To the terrifying torrent to our souls the deep
Of "terrorism" unleashes? It goes on and on...
Rolling over minds and souls; the picture seems to darken.
Yet when seen from depths of faith one knows that gone
Is what is one's own sense of Presence. So we harken
To our pray'rs, our people...here we garner stay...
Here we harbor hope...in this is Love Divine and peace
enfolding.
And when we've done all this we'll have all the grace
We need to stare into the lion's mouth rejoicing
While in the lion's den our full jail-term's length.
(Don't you think that Daniel's plight was unexpected?)
Yes, "terrorism" is a word that beats one's strength...
Grown men rant and rave all day unrelentingly.
It is as though they're forced into complete submission
To the fear within their heart's and soul's inner workings.
And where in here is love, Divine Love, in its completion?
It drives out fear with all its evil, everywhere evil's lurking...
And where there's love, there's joy in all its fullness...

It is to these I turn with all their peace and inner quiet...
Here is strength, faith, hope, and charity with wellness.
Can you believe it? How could you help but not deny it?
Dear Lord and Father of these, Your little ones who've found it...
Your Love, Your Peace and Joy—please give it
To those who seem to have lost it.
Amen.

February 25, 2006
Saturday of the 7th Week of Ordinary Time

On pain and evil, after discussing it in Bible study in relation to the reading of the Letters of John 1, 2, and 3 and also the Book of Habbukuk…

When one is ready to shout out loudly, "No more!"
When trials seem overwhelming; and all is fright…
One remembers Jesus and the apostles in the storm…
Jesus said, "Peace, be still…" and all was quiet in the night…
Love is that centering which calms the central core;
It is the Holy Spirit making the blackest blackness "white."
One could not believe and say that all this is lore,
And yet there's Truth here; and that is Love requites.
To understand it in its fullness, we Christians will implore
That sacrifice, yes, blood and martyrdom (which befrights)
Is gift required for that peace. So Jesus died for
Us to save, and Love was His unending sight.
And Jesus, Himself, said He was God's own Son; poor
Though He was on Earth—yet He had God's full love-might.
Jesus was God's own sacrifice of Love; so we adore
All that He is—Everlasting Love and Life—the delights
Which we claim and God gives eternally. Before
You desist and give way to evil's bitter blight—
Remember that God has in mind only goodness. More
Than even this, God will make ALL Love's rule right…
"My God, my God; why have You abandoned me?" we roar!
(Our hearts are in tune with Jesus!) We search for light
Around us in the darkness—and only then we begin to soar
Toward heaven! God has given us wings to mount the heights!

It is to Paradise and divinity that we are fully borne!
Then the Sun burns most gloriously! Entirely white-bright!
And we are privy to the most memorable morning Light.
(And then what fire of love in us we see that God ignites!)

March 11, 2006
Saturday of the First Week of Lent

I heard the knock…yet it did not seem to me that
There could be Love so unconditionally free and constant…

I haven't believed…because nothing seemed
Real enough to convince me God could truly Be…

I couldn't love…because I have hurt so much
God is only a distant entity as such…

God is for the emotionally broken…
I am among the intellectually awakened…

Are you among these? Those for whom
God is a faraway or unreal deity for another to consume
For reasons unknown to or beneath you? There is yet
A journey inward far more telling and intelligent
Than you will ever guess… You have only to confess
That you do not know all—
For there is One Who Is…
And for you there's a call…
You'll hear it when? Must God insist?

March 22, 2006
Wednesday of the 3rd Week of Lent

I heard a child crying this morning while at prayer,
Which brought to mind the thought of those holy tears—
The living water of our immolation that brings us near
To Christ within—the tears of perfect contrition. No fears
Of punishment or hell will take us there—it's Love alone,
God, Himself, in all His Mighty Glory and Awesomeness,
Who sweeps us to this poverty of self and soul,
Which fills our emptiness and swells our littleness
So God in wanton Love and abandonment bowls
Us over in return for our loving forgetfulness...
So when the skies rain down heavenly abundance,
And the children cry because they must stay inside,
I remember the transformation of the waters as such—
And know in the face of sorrow is another tomorrow
Where agonies become victories and it doesn't hurt as much...
So, dear Jesus, Your Way becomes mine as I give up
All my pride and all that is mine. I will drink Your Cup,
Watch the rain fall, and eat the banquet that is Your Sup
While the nations begin their transformation...
Thy Kingdom Come; Thy Will Be Done.

March 23, 2006
Thursday of the 3rd Week of Lent

On thinking of the "consumer society"…on thinking of what it means to be an apostle to the "consumer society"…

If I am to be a consumer, let it only to be of God:
Of all His Ways—to be His People, to do His Will—
That's for me, this humble and eccentric "broad"!
Let me be empty—but not with earthly treasures fill…
I want to be so empty that I can fill myself full of Him
Who is the Eternal and Everlasting and Who will
Not wear out to be thrown away when light grows dim—
Because His Light never does… He always thrills!
He ALWAYS satisfies until I need nothing else! Can
Anything you imagine do this—all the sex, drugs, money,
Food, alcohol, or power create feelings so real that last?
When you think about these things you'll notice: it's funny,
But all of those temporary good feelings turn sour somehow.
All those addictions we have are really idols of sorts…
Of course, we know this deep inside, but lose control. Now
Lost without Love we wander looking to numb and to soothe.
O God, You know I'm only looking for You!
"Love Divine, All Love Compelling"
Take my heart, and give it to Jesus, Your Son,
Who walked on Earth; Who died on Earth. This impelling
Story can be uniquely ours—we are transformed and won
Over by a Beauty, Truth, and Love so profound
It shakes us to our very ground…
And we are FOUND!
Blessed be God Forever!

March 31, 2006
Friday of the Fourth Week of Lent

On Galatians 4:4-7 and the way some of the new translations substitute "gender inclusive" words like "child" for "son" in THESE critical readings—completely distorting the meanings for me, greedy though I may be for ALL the gifts Christ has won for me, yet also grateful and wanting to give Him thanks for EVERYTHING! A Eucharistic meditation...

Dear Savior, I want to most truly confess
That by words we are both cursed and blessed.
May these words bring You glory...
And tell one kind of story...
Of Your Most Magnificent Mysteriousness...

The living Christ Who is THE SON,
And through Him everything was won
When He accepted Calvary
And died on that awe-full tree
But was raised from death for you and me
So we could be free
And be borne to divinity.

We, ourselves, as our mortal lot
Cannot find Him, but us He sought.
The mark He places on our souls
Is a deep, dark mysterious kind of hole
Only He can fill. We try and cajole
All sorts of stymieing substitutes—
Sex, drugs, power, "things"—but they all "lose"

Or we replace Him with questions
And answers galore—need I mention
Atheism, relativism, secularism,
Materialism, escapism, and nihilism,
To name but a few. These leave
Us with a chill (yes, we who believe)
And yet there remains a fever in our minds...
Why are so many people so increasingly blind
To the immense power of that Divine Love—
Which was so freely given with His Blood?
What human today would give her/his life
So another might have sanctity? The strife
And disbelief associated with that sacrifice
Of perfect and holy love—or is disbelief simple
Self-absorption or neglectful
Willfulness brought on by arrogance—
These we can fairly well understand
Because we, too, hold up our hands
As common and ordinary sinning types—
Yet we also hold our breath—no "hype"
Here intended, because we pray with all strength
That the grace of that same Jesus will remain
On these human words to convince just one,
That they, too, are "son" and have won
Through Him the self-same divinity
To which He and, therefore, in His name we
Are borne as well. Jesus is NOT daughter nor child
Of God, but Son. It is His very substance—beguiled
Not by neuter words—I am gifted to be by the Creator.
And not I alone, but humankind, reinstated
In humankind's splendor by pristine Christ the Sun—
Source of all hope, rays of all forgiving heat,

Fires of Divine Love toward which we all run.
In Him alone we will not find defeat.
The inheritance is ALL—it was given in trust.
The Creator asks that you accept it as such
Because the cross is included—by which it was won.
But Christ—humanity's Aviator—has only just begun!
He spoke to His Creator Father as "Abba," as an intimate
And in humility as a lovely toddler baby—limited
As He was by His earthly body but knowing
And growing as the son of a flesh-bound mother
(Herself graced with all Divine favor—another
Better the Creator could never have created.)
To this intimacy we are initiated wholly and completely.
By His Incarnation He accomplished a miracle so neatly—
Tied us to the Creator as a parent and the Parent knows
Our mortal lot succinctly... (at least, we understand it so)
Again, just what was meant whereby this Son we were feted?
And we intend to be in on what He has intended!
A union of spirits...in spiritual marriage...communion
Sublime of perfect Love, Truth, and Beauty...fusion
With All-In-All (are you pulled to this call?) We are hewn
From Christ's substance—His "Son-ship" through
Adoption by God in Christ. This is not meant for a few
But it is meant for us ALL—that is what is meant
By the "fullness of the Kingdom." We are bent
On its coming; and are not to stall because it's already won.
Although we live it out uniquely it is ours as community—
Together forever—we as Christ's Body are all ONE. Be
Mystery in complexity; in completeness is unity. We see
In each other the divinity called forth wondrously...
Is it greed: our wanting what was ours from time
Immemorial...not to refuse that which is not rescinded?

We only want to show you the treasures and remind
You of what is lacking in case there's been a call
And a decision that was yours—and that's the wall
To this glorious and sublime message you're learning
Which has no ending and isn't one of your earning.
To those we offer a welcome and a place of peace
With a heavenly love that quenches thirst, and that never ceases.
To others who've not had the "call" we unendingly pray
Knowing the Creator answers these requests every way.
May you be struck with these words, and pray every day
That Christ's love will envelope you, too, so you'll become
A "son" and an heir to God's Immensity soon. And the love
That you seek will not be found up above, but in your heart...
And you'll know the sure peace Christ always imparts...
For those who do not know their "son-ship—" for those for whom
God is not an intimate, loving parent. Through Christ may you soon
See all that you can inherit on Earth and beyond. No doom
Or gloom can ever remain because at this "inn there's always room."
"Come and see" for yourself...

April 7, 2006
Friday of the Fifth Week of Lent

My father has a little robin that "hangs around" him all of the time… It follows him as he goes about his yard work and is often on the chain-link fence near the back gate in the morning when I get up… Somehow I needed to write a tribute to this little fellow, who is so trusting…

My Father's Garden-Buddy…

My father has a robin friend who simply waits
For him each morning perched firmly on the fence.
Dad digs earthworms and little bugs—their earthly fates
Are sweetmeats for his "garden buddy." Let
No one laugh…this loving bird follows
Dad around and seems so surely trusting.
It's food for thought: we complex folk, callow
And discouraged though we sometimes be—if we sing
To God for security, God will feed us with impunity.

April 14, 2006
Good Friday

My father just gave me a book to peruse on the former "secrets" of freemasonry (they are no longer "secrets," being open to all by way of publication—but this book refers to "secret scrolls of Jesus.") There is also media sensation around a "Gospel of "Judas," which has been hidden from sight. "What to make of it?" asks Dad...

On "secrets" and salvation...

I only wish to say and exclaim, "My dear papa, oh, no!"
The way to salvation is and always has been
Perfectly open and unhidden for each to live and grow.
The books of Scripture, the ordinary path to win
Salvation, are those used by folk the most...
And contain certain and honest Truth. To begin,
It is our hearts, within us, which are hidden; ghosts
Here reside in a deep hole in them—the seat where sin
Is let in because we fill it with pride when we, as hosts,
Should let God be here instead... We are to be children,
Little and unassuming—open and humble—putting aside
All ideas of "special" and extraordinary. It is then
We learn of the exalted. These facts we do not hide—
The "occult" is always suspect here. Why were they
Forgotten in the first place? Because in them Truth does not lie...
Truth is Light and found in the Light. Christ is the Way.
He died openly and publicly—like the Truth He IS—
Naked on the cross, exposed to ALL, in utter humility.
Secrets? I hardly think so...and naked we go to our finish...

What to do with all these "forces" that could bring us to our knees?
Bring them to the Light of Day... The One Who Does Not
Diminish...
The Sun of God! Whose healing rays bring health and hope, keys
To our understanding of our salvation which IS and WAS
And EVER WILL BE! AMEN!

April 17, 2006
Easter Monday

On thinking of a suicide in an assisted living facility in which I
ministered several months ago. In sadness…

When clouds are hovering; when covered is the sun;
If blackness is nearing even in your human mind—
Remember,"fleetness" is how the race is won…
Like antelopes, or quick deer, or scriptural "hinds"—
The word for this is "run," "run," "Run," "RUN!"
As fast as you can—straight for the Immaculate SUN!
WHO IS RISEN for you; WHO CONQUERED the grave!
He and He only will be able to save!
In His deep love you He will keep;
Safe from all harm—freely to weep…
So run very fast…
Into His arms—as fast as you can!
Jesus is Lord!
Let Him be adored!

April 17, 2006
Easter Monday

So many things "point the way" to me these days—the simple and "ordinary…" As I ponder St. Therese's "little way," I am so struck with the "little things" and the messages I get from my mentors to stick with the "ordinary." I, myself, had become attached to the "big and exalted." So these "little and ordinary" have become very appealing, as God has shown me lately how tiring the others are…

Yes, Lord, indeed You are Grand and Exalted, as Mighty You Be!
But, dear and Holy One, I, myself, am little and stuck in poverty;
Poverty in mind and soul gives me room to fill with All You Are;
The tears flow in plenty as I contemplate You among the stars!
Yet, my Light, when I am silent and at home in ordinary times
I find You here in the persons and things around me, if I'm not blind.
So, my Esteemed and Awesome Friend, keep me supple and open
To Your manifestations in this world of Yours; no token
Of Your Love too little not to notice…nothing too broken
Nor too covered-over with earthly grime to forget to see
As You see—forgivingly and with charity, forever into eternity.
And "ordinary" is really the way to this blessed fraternity…

May 15, 2006
Vigil of the Fifth Sunday in Easter

On that fruitfulness and flowering that May brings, so reminiscent of the Blessed Mother whom we honor this month…

My dear protectress and mother, Blessed Virgin Mary, who stands
Beneath the cross of her Blessed Son, our Redeemer and Lord,
Jesus. I'll assume there were no flowers there on that sweet land
On which you stood, side-by-side with St. John, who adored
Your Son like you, my dear mistress… Yet strewn with love
And blossoms of fairest loyalty to God, Himself, the pathway
Straight to Paradise was pointed out by the sacrificial blood
And water you witnessed pouring out of His pierced side. Lay
No crown of roses on His brow—the thorns already stay! Yet now
You, O mother of fruitfulness and Wondrous Gift, have more to say!
"Believe in Him!" "He IS risen from the dead!" "Alleluia!" "Allow
The words to truly fill your hearts with grace and joy! With Him let us
Triumph over every evil in our lives—no suffering to fill us with contempt
Or even strife… For Christ has conquered all that holds and keeps us
In the grave. With Him we have strength to heal and to be brave…" Lent
Has passed with Lenten poverty—to bring us Spring-time hope and fecundity.
Dear St. Mary, you who have blessed us with your Sacred Maternity…
"Pray for us now and at the hour of our death…"

May 28, 2006
Ascension Sunday

My religious mentor reminded me today to be open to all God's gifts on an ongoing basis…be aware and always open for surprises…I realized I have also asked for the cross—because I feel Jesus close when I am suffering, too, and feel I am doing something for humankind in this way. Today I have had glimpses of my cross on and off…and have "offered it up."

Today I know so intimately that my cross is also gift—
How crass, you might say! Are you some sort of hypochondriac?
The Lord asks my sufferings always up to Him highly lift—
It's only in this way that He can see where these sufferings truly stack…
Have you given Him all you can as your earthly duties go…
Have you loved your neighbors enough in the ways your life has shown?

Today my aches and pains have bothered until I knew that they weren't mine…
I gave them up to Jesus—to be offered for bread and wine
Of His table, which are His Body and Blood—I added mine to His for love
Of humankind and all its sins. This gift I know He accepted…for I'm kin—
I'm His son like Christ—this divinely-inspired is His Word altogether.
And is and will be forever, and ever. And the Son is the sign.

So what gift we get today is always a miracle in the happening to be.
It is a matter to behold—and in the perceiving and believing—we
don't know
What is in store from day to day. Yet to let one's mind go free
And surrender one's body, too, to the Almighty One within. Show
The Lord He's King—let the anthems ring! Then He'll light your fires
And kindle your desires…because your passions flame higher
and higher!

And on some days the gifts are more earthly-minded. Rooted in ground
They are ordinary in form and mode—yet quite extraordinary in
scope…
When we look we see them all around—everywhere we look
they're found!
So open your eyes and ears to be sensitive—feel your body and be
open to hope—
God's gifts are present and fulminating in abundance—they help
us to cope.

So if God chooses to gift me extraordinarily I will His offering be…
Yet the little things please me mightily—because in them I, too,
Him see.
Not for me to desire what He wills to give—because consolations
are not
For what I look—pleasures of my Bounteous Creator become loss
When sought—because I'm always seeking better. No, the cross
Is what I seek because that was Jesus' gift to me. When sought
Like this—my gift to Him and thee—I become ONE with ONE
BUT THREE!

June 1, 2006
St. Justin, Martyr

On gratitude...

After meditating on those boundless gifts of heaven, O Lord,
That are ours from You with immense and overflowing love,
Gratitude wells like a torrential river—cuts like a sword
Into any leftover self-centeredness on my part—placed above
All fleshly concerns because of its power and grace. Feel
The impact of Your giving-ness and tenderness! Your desire
To please me—though in no way have I earned it—real
Enough it is, however! O Gracious and Merciful One—fire
That this gratitude is—it fills my soul with holiness and need.
Your desire for me totally fuels me with complaisance.
Your merest wish for me to do is what I want, too. So seed
The future with Your Will—but pray, have it make sense
To my mortal mind so clarity is provided in Your Will
So I not stray. I want only to give You glory in all I do!
For Paradise and Your Face is where I will ever view
Your Will—for Your work in me, although not through
(And I am always aware that I am being wooed by You...),
Is all throughout with Your Essence fulfilled and imbued.
In gratitude...

July 2, 2006
Sunday of the Thirteenth Week of Ordinary Time

God's incredible sense of humor has been displayed with such amazing alacrity this last week I am truly astonished... Being the author of it, however, I should not be—for this suggests a degree of human self-aggrandizement for which I have shame—why do we not recognize God's sense of humor?

I, for one, know I take myself far too seriously—
And You have told me so again and again, O Lord...
You'd play me for a fool and have me SEEM to be
A blooming idiot instead of that which is adored...
Because I know humility and light-heartedness
Are encapsulated in all holiness...
(Yes, another word for wholeness) and strength
And health are part of what You bless.
I know Jesus came and joked; he laughed at length
With His disciples and friends because laughter
Which is joyfulness pleases You, dear Father...
This past week has seen Your humor—softer
Than rainwater—but richer than fruitcake—rather
Better than any I've ever seen or heard from humans
Anywhere I've visited... O Loved One, to display
This kind of humor that can illuminate and enliven
Simple humanity so they can begin to stay
The course of their harried lives wearing silly grins
On careworn faces—THIS, TOO, IS YOUR ESSENCE!
Father, forgive me my many, many faults and sins!
Then transcendence is sheer luminescence!

July 7, 2006
Friday of the 13th Week of Ordinary Time

The priest at Mass today said that evil is the ABSENCE of God (an Augustine concept according to another learned friend of mine). This brings up for me many interesting concepts to ponder... (and for those in inquiry classes at RCIA pithy questions like "Did God create evil?" would seem to be helped by this—but is it?) I only know that many of these questions, which can cause crisis for some—are super-ceded for me by the assurance that out of everything WILL COME GOOD! This abiding hope has even been demonstrated for me in my life again and again...

Oh the message of that cross upon which the Son of God hung—
On which all evil and all maliciousness and hate came together.
The workings could never be more clear—the soundings have rung
From steeples and towers of all nations in most inclement weather
In warning... "It's here! It's here that your heads must be turning!
Have you not seen or heard the stern clarion call of the angel hordes?
The love of God implores your most important lessons of learning...
The use of your life—from cradle to death—is the ultimate award
And also the instrument of your deliverance and resurrection—
No lie! To lose the chance of a lifetime to win salvation eternal
And the keys to Paradise—your fingertips at your election...
Seems incredibly stubbornly false and moronic. My most maternal
Heart turns softly tender because I know that each "evil" we encounter
In this trial-filled life (it is made so that we will grow able and strong...)
Can be, with God's amazing assistance, made into "goodness" if we want to

Imitate Christ's Passion… There is no doubt that this is a difficult, long,

Spiritually-heavy path for most (yet, do we not know "my yoke is easy, My burden, light"?…) So we must be cautious about that which we call

"Evil"—not to give that which is God's discipline, or trials meant to be Tests for our betterment a twist that's not meant—or even there at all…

In this misidentification we bring "evil" into the world ourselves as I see.

But I am only a lowly and miserably simple "little one" whose faults Lie around calling sin that which is not—according to my confessors—

That which I have choice therein—is not what I was confessing…

There are matters better taken to spiritual direction, I now know… These involve those "original sin" traits in order to help us worthily grow.

My own brand of "evil"—and related they are; which should be quite clear…

And I am meaning to share these most delicate of God's lessons… With you, my friends and readers, to eat with joy the fruits that near Your hands from the tree of experience—mine…and be blessed to know

There's a little less "evil" lurking around than perhaps you thought…

So don't say the name if it's not merited… (it'll come soon enough if so…)

In the name of Jesus Christ these words are hewn and wrought… By me…

September 30, 2006
St. Jerome

There is so much about oneself that always is in need of "fixing"…one is always "falling short" in so many ways so apparent to oneself and others, too. Sin is rampant and visible—and one could be taking oneself to task at all times—focused on all those things, always working to "improve" those things that need it… Confession is so necessary and helpful. And when one gets to even the basis of "original sin"—one would hope this ever-present "searching" could begin to end. But it doesn't until realized is…at the basis of it is this central "fact"—Jesus' mercy—which is the ground of Christian hope and joy…

It seems I'm not "empty" enough…too "proud," too "loud,"
Too "fast," deceitful, and sometimes full of enmity besides…
What else could I throw into the pot? I'll join the crowd
As common and ordinary sinner—and yet a total believer
In the mercy of my Lord, Jesus Christ. So to Him I throw
Open the windows of my soul and show that I'm a receiver
Of all the Love He has to offer. So, running quickly I'll go
Faster and faster to His pierced, draining side—as water
And blood pour down in recognition of the toil He
And I have merited as we wend our way to the Father.
No, my cross is not as His was—but I have joined them prayerfully
Hoping He will accept mine as an offer in pain and suffering—
For my own and the world's benefit—as He sees fit…
And if you cannot see how anything similar—remembering
Nothing like it in your experience—could be of benefit…
Let it be known—I have nothing else to offer this world but pain…

If I can bear it graciously and lovingly so that another will not
Have to do so—may my little gift be that one's life's gain...
I may be doing so for you—so that you may not be caught
In a trial too heavy for you to bear...a life too fraught
With accidents and illnesses that bring you to naught...
But these crosses brought me to Jesus—were it He you sought...

October 3, 2006
Tuesday of the 26ᵗʰ Week of Ordinary Time

Emboldened by a fellow poet's words that my poetry seemed to be "too much" as though I was not "caught up", but observing myself in the process—I immediately sensed what he was intending by those words…for I have known that this relationship with God is so intimate and personal I have used other's words for fear of "leaking" something notoriously beyond what I wanted "out there"…

O my dear God: My Playmate, My Soul-mate, Whose Arms
Surround me with most loving compassion and warmth beyond measure!
Let's play on my bed—where pain and crosses of agony would alarm
Some, but not You—the Son of the most simple and tender of creatures…
Who lights my passions with the fire of fervor unreservedly
(In fact, to the point that some feel it must be wrongfully felt
Or somehow misguided or misspent…) O woefully hurriedly
I awaken to find You beside me—again issuing strength
For the day with the self-same passions assuredly bent not to stay
Or delay me in finding You in ALL the day's demands. But on my bed,
In my most intimate hours, my prayers, You come to awaken me
To the excitement of Your certainty. Yes, we are wed;
And so the scriptures said—"Beloved… You are my delight."
Though I not find You in the night—I know You are there—because You
Promised me so… O Master of Every Want and Need, no fright
Will ever overtake me long—for You supply me with ALL before

You're through!

I only have to look around! On the counterpanes I lie for the pain of ills

And handicaps, yet joy comes plentifully in the midst of prayer and supplication

From the One-Who-Gives-All to the one-who-needs-all. Deathly still

I try to be in hopes that jubilation will overcome me in Your creation—

Of-new-making. Ongoing hope seasons those who wait for God's Will.

And I never tire of even the seeming unending dreaming of this: Your Love

To empty me of all that I am—so I am only full of You and You only. As such

I long to be completely one with You—Body, Mind, Soul, and Blood...

Outdone, overtaken, overwhelmed, and overrun...

Must I struggle on earth to give up all of me—or

Will death be the door to the prize to be won?

This ultimate union precludes even seeing Your Holy Face

Because caught in ALL-in-ALL I've become that sacred place

Of Eternity's Love-Making in God's Almighty Embrace...

October 31, 2006
Vigil of All Saints Day

An assignment of a tutor to write a short Psalm in varying poetical styles, meters, and rhyme schemes...

Psalm 123—in Free-flowing Rhyme

O God, enthroned above in heavens high,
I lift my eyes up—=seeking You...
Not so unlike the eyes of slaves who lie
Awaiting master's bidding by hands that cue...
We, too, are slave to You. We anticipate
Your keen pity, my Lord, to strike us through.
For those who show us scorn have long worn
Leers of meanest complacency.
Have pity, Lord; have pity...

Psalm 123—Haiku

O God in heaven...   Contemptible me!
Me, a contemptible slave—   Who lifts seeking eyes to Thee—
Pity for leaven!   Your Sov'reign pity...

              Slave I feel to be...
              In Your service I do seek
              Your holy pity...

Psalm 123—Iambic Pentameter

O God, enthroned above in heavens grand,
As I lift up my eyes to seek Your Face,
I think of slaves who look for masters' hands
Which cue, which indicate each subtle demand.

Our eyes, therefore, are fixed upon the Lord
In hopes of pity, simple pity, for award.

Your pity, Yahweh, is our only hope.
For we have had our share of scorn and jeers,
Complacency shatters/ we can't cope!
We come to you in grieving and in tears…

Our eyes, therefore, are fixed upon the Lord
In hopes of pity, simple pity, for award.

October 31, 2006
Vigil of All Saints Day

Psalm 123—as a Shakespearean Sonnet

O God, enthroned in highest heavenly light—
I lift my eyes to you like the humblest slave
Who waits for human master's sheer delight—
Obedience by hand-signs, bond to grave.
My mistress's merest glance immediately
Rebukes my sloth; I come most willingly.
To You, O Lord, these servant kin bring need.
In Greatness find compassion in Your pity.
Pity, Lord, is what we ask of You…
We have been subject of the jeers and scorn
Complacent folk place at our feet as due.
Will You abide as losses are wept and mourned?
Your pity, Lord, Your pity seek we here…
Without it we have only dark and fears.

Psalm 123—as Free Verse

O God, enthroned above
In heavenly light,
I lift my eyes to You.

Not so unlike the slave
Who intently watches
His earthly master for cues
On what it is
He is to do...

Or the servant maid
Eyeing her mistress
Through veils of gossamer—
For the slightest turn
Of her hand...

I am so intent on pleasing You...

Now I ask You for pity—

We are subject
To jeers and scorn
Of the proud—the complacent...

You, Lord, are Almighty,
Your pity is what I ask...
I lift my eyes to You.

November 1, 2006
All-Saints' Day

Psalm 123—Haiku

Command me, O Lord,
But give me simple pity—
Generous reward…

My aching heart seeks
Where my eyes lift to see Thee—
An offer: pity…

Slave though I may be,
I seek to glimpse Your Glory
Pour forth Your pity…

Obedience is…
Where the aching heart doth live.
Rule me with pity.

The proud jeer and scorn…
O Highest Lord pity me
For I weep and mourn.

O God, pity me.
The proud in complacency
Scorn us viciously…

November 1, 2006
All-Saints' Day

Psalm 123—A Haiku

The proud heap jeers, scorn…
From on high, O Sovereign Lord,
Pity me, forlorn…

As a Shakespearean Sonnet…

O God, Who Is in highest dwelling places,
I lift my eyes to search for Your compassion…
For I am but a lowly humble slave
Obediently watching in my fashion.
Your slightest whim is my command, O Lord—
Desire to please is where my heart resides.
Please to succor me with just reward…
For complacent people scorn us in their pride.
Their leers and jeers scorch deeply in my heart;
And You, My Lord, deliver pity soothing me.
Your pity, humble pity, travels far.
For little else I ask, Almighty Thee.
In lowliness I long to see Your Face.
O pity me—and give me this one grace.

November 3, 2006
St. Martin de Porres

As I was reading the writings of St. John of the Cross last night I was so struck with a stanza describing his sorrow at seeing the Blessed Sacrament. This stanza I contrast with another statement he makes later, "God does not will us to suffer." I know, of course, this stanza is NOT describing suffering, but a "wound of love", which is NOT suffering because of a "detachment" from suffering that he has with the grace of God attained. Because this particular kind of wound is not a wound from which one suffers as such—but considering the use of the word "sorrow" for seeing the Sacrament—which is for many of us an action of great bliss...

O Dear God, Author of the Greatest Gifts
Which You dole out mercifully to all of us—
Great and little. You must notice how we lift
Them up to You... And I heartily suspect
Our earnestness in use plays an important part
In how we notice them in each other, too.
Grant that Your Presence ply my heart
Like St. John of the Cross... If only You
Would be received by my soul as beautifully
As with St. Therese of Lisieux...

But I am me... Your searching fires beckon far
Less loftily now with me—a crone who limps
And moans most ordinarily... No star
Of fame or fortune shares its home with me,
But dare I accept those gifts You offer freely
Because with gratitude abounding for the love

I feel so graciously You have given—no, not elevated
To union of unknowing or not understanding...
Beyond words... My devotion is simply that.
And as I sit and meditate before You—landing
In the midst of grandest understanding is this...
You are just as pleased with simple prayer—
Offered with sincere soul-felt honesty as the bliss
Of highest ecstasy. You love no more
The exalted saint than the little unnoticed one
Kneeling near Your feet. Only You, for
Whom I long for perfect union—
Without true knowledge of what I'm asking,
In reality. Gratitude for what I've been given
Already makes me hesitate...perhaps
This is not where I am meant to go—the plan
Doesn't include my being here... (Yet, so,
Have I drawn back from His love in any way
That has precluded the fullness of His Presence
In my life, in my soul, in my prayer this day?)
I know You only reciprocate with deepest love...
It is I, simply I, who hold myself up.
This necessary question lightens my earthly sentence
Of cares and woes and other troubles and blows...
For it fills me full of possibilities and probabilities...
And lets go of strife and wear...
How to make this more clear?
I cannot and do not suffer anymore—
In spite of cruel pain, family woes, financial blows—
There is no real suffering because I gave it all to love
Of You and Yours. Yet this IS the cup
I promised You in perpetuity.
It is very rich, this cup, yet...

It is not the whole picture—it is what I share with Thee…
Am I making myself victim—instead of opening to Your bounty?
(Even beyond Eucharist in which Your substance makes me Thee)
I now am emboldened and ask most rashly—
Will You denude my soul enough to marry me spiritually?
As You have formally taken my hand in wedlock,
May I be all Yours? Strengthen me as a rock
For this monumental request. That I never block
The totality of Your Towering Love from my life…
That those remnants of my personality giving strife
To my prayer be removed…and Your Joyful Entrance
To my temple be praised and glorified; ever since
Its consecration this temple is building the Kingdom
Of Jesus Christ through the grace of the Creator/Holy Spirit.
And I—for the active and pre-eminent Presence I long
To be over-whelmed in union and totally filled-up…
Whatever the cost or cross—this martyrdom of having
And self-seeking I greet wholly humbly…
All for Thee…

Yet, this may not be Your Will—and not come to be…
For all is gift—and at Your Sovereign Hand I have come to see
In gratitude, too, is certain bliss. To be just ordinarily
Yours (even my consecration has its ordinary overtones…)
Is also vocation blessed and sanctified in saintly measure.
And how I wish to tell Your people that this is so!
A hierarchy of holiness brings You no pleasure;
For You wish ALL Your people to be GOLD!
Each in his/her own station and road—unique or plain—
This is God's Way…
So I wait…
All for Thee…

November 7, 2006
Tuesday of the 31st Week of OT

On, once again, pondering the mysteries of "infinite variety" in God's People...how God loves each and every unique one uniquely and equally; and how God doles out gifts equally, too— but our gifts look different and are meant for different ends.

A hierarchy of holiness—
(Which is a bitter pill to swallow)
This is not to God's own eyes
A golden road to follow...
For each and every one of us
Has gifts and wholeness inherent.
It's finding Jesus in us that Truth's
Most wondrous miracle will merit.

So to St. John of the Cross—
In seeing the Sacrament found sorrow...
(reminded him of having not...)
While some have perfect happiness.
And Dear Therese, Little Flower,
Sacrifice—renunciation
Brought sweetness to her heart;
But for many these bring conflagration.

Jesus taught us to pray, "Do not put us
To the test." Yet St. John (yes, again)
Teaches "the test brings union." Truth
Be known—we are all different sorts.
It is in finding peace with God inside
Whatever the situation—that matters most.

November 7, 2006
Tuesday of the 31st Week of OT

Psalm 150—in free verse (unrhymed)—with freely-chosen underlying structure

O praise God in His Mighty Majesty!
Praise Him with all you are able!
For He is great and has done marvelous deeds—
Worthy of the highest praise of angels and saints...
Let us praise Him on the golden trumpets...
Let their loud fanfare precede the lyres and the harps
Which the angelic hosts pluck in joyful harmony...
We feast eyes on the heavenly throng...
Praising God with all they are able.
Soon in line come the cymbals crashing...
Triumphantly soaring the pipers piping
Join the ranks of fit dancers leaping...
All the earth breathe the praise of the Lord!
Swelling songs of praise to our Master and King,
We praise Him with all we are able.

In free-choice of structure and rhyme scheme

Our Mighty God—we praise You!
O'er H'ven and Earth You rule us...
Your thrilling deeds compel us...
With angelic hosts we praise You!

Power of Powers—we praise You!
In the vault of heaven and within us
Your greatness resides forever...
On our knees we praise You!

On trumpets golden we praise You!
The lyres and harps adoring
Praise Your Great and Holy Name...
In row after row we praise You!

With tambourines shaking we praise You!
We dance to pipes and strings
In praise as we worship...
With a loud cymbal crash—we praise You!

Let all be an instrument of praise in their worship...
As we breathe His Praise to the Cosmos for His Glory!—Alleluia

November 13, 2006
St. Francis Xavier Cabrini

I'm still thinking of St. John of the Cross's "wound of love" that afflicted him with "sorrow" upon seeing the Blessed Sacrament...

Becoming so absorbed in gratitude...
It leads to bliss...
Because now I know my God
Who gives like this.
Wondering if...
God leaves my personhood intact,
My ego where it is...
To be able to give
The bounty of that gratitude
Back again to Him...

November 15, 2006
St. Albert

O Hidden God, though I sense You not,
I know Your Secret Presence—and it guides
Through these rocky spaces in which I'm caught.
A thick veil between us, and in darkness plunged
My weary soul. Yet the blackness is lightening in fright
Before Your altar and in Your dwelling place.
O Blessed Sacrament—in seeing You, I, too,
Now feel the sorrow St. John of the Cross has taught
Was his on seeing You. For days have gone
In restlessness and seeking You in prayer;
But I've not found—and have been in grueling pain.
My body and mind are crosses I have borne
In love—this I've dared for You, my King,
but You want more…
And since my life is free to love You still,
If You want this too, Lord, I give it unto Thee…
It, too, can be my wooden cross to bear. But if Your Will
Is that my life be spared, I ask, dear Father, simply
Not to leave me—except to strengthen. And I know, too,
That if You ask these crosses of me—in the end
I'll always flee to Thee in heaven above…
    Above these trials…
        above these crosses…
            above this pain…
Where You await with opened arms in almighty LOVE;
And there I'll stay in eternity where JOY remains…

November 15, 2006
St. Albert

Psalm 150 per Emily Dickinson…

O Praise God—Mighty Majesty!
Praise Him in His Power and Greatness!
With a trumpet blast—Holy!
And the lute and harp—with zest!
Tambourines and dancing;
Heavenly prancing!
The strings and pipes bring
Music fancy…
While the cymbals crashing
Punctuate the breathing
All for Him…
The Holy One!
Praise the Lord! Alleluia!

November 16, 2006
St. Gertrude

This particular saint is one of my favorites; I have been highly influenced by her writings in my interior and prayer life... Today I think of my Lord in my darkness—and know that He will come again...

Where You're hidden, Holy One,
in magnificence, I cannot find—
I search; I wander; I feel undone...
My stomach churns; my legs unwind—
It's only You, Who are my Guide...
I know You're near me: oh, so close—
And yet I doubted—believe me, Lord,
These thoughts alarmed me! But though I know
Spiritual journeys sometimes bring
Trials aplenty—so I have hope...
The sweet perfusion of this faith sings
Through the deep of darkness' keep...
The lesson of Your lovingness
Permeates my soul as pain creeps in.
I truly wondered if I am fit
To partake of You in Eucharist...
Once again, I hear Your voice afar...
"Take...eat..." and know You do not bar=—
For You have healed the sins of mine—
This trial intends, instead, another star...
That guides me home to You in heaven.
The agonies that are so dear—are not just madness—
But clearly fair—for we are sinful (all of us)
And must prepare for heaven's blessedness

In the fires of purity and
He gives such peace and joy in hope—thankfulness.
To those who love in all of this...
Darkness is pure gift...

December 23, 2006
Third Saturday of Advent

Before the Blessed Sacrament...

O humble Jesus, I come to You...
In the white host before me, I give due
All that You are... Yet silent I stay
Because Your Greatness awes me this way.
That simple, white bread that's human-made
Nourishes with bliss beyond physical frame's
Ability to contain—my love so unafraid
And impassioned by Your Presence therein
I weep for sheer joy. Yet peace, when
My heart longs for rest, is also aware...
Knowledge of You is transmitted wordlessly: bare.
My agitating mind "let's go" in surrender...
Quietly, quietly my soul opens:
waiting for You to enter...

January 2, 2007

This was started while meditating in front of the Blessed Sacrament several days ago—and forgotten… I find it on the back of my daily prayer list now—resurrect it—and begin to rethink it…

Yes, Lord, seek and take…all I have; it's Yours…
My memory, my intellect, even my will…
This holy stripping I must undergo
All for You—my desire thrills
To be so blessed by You I'm known
This intimately for eternity.
No renunciation too stringent; too painful
For joy this bountiful. Be
Gifted with my gratitude,
Sweet Lord (in You I dwell with peace
Beyond all imagining.) Silence
Greets my heartbeats
Drumming cadences of love songs
Quietly—quietly…
Wanting only You—deep in the core of me—
That hidden secret erupts into ecstasy
So that now I want to shout it endlessly:
Jesus! Blessed Jesus, My King!
You Who Did the Holy Spirit Bring!
Of the Creator—Let Our Praises Sing!
O Holy Trinity! One-Yet-Three!
Let our anthems in triumph ring!
To be so consumed by You, my Lord—
That Your Substance becomes mine…
And yet I am not consumed—I, too, am divine.

This is my call and promise—the "why"
Of my purpose... No other sign
Needed... Here is the "high"
To which we attain...nigh...

January 21, 2007
Third Sunday in Ordinary Time

O Blessed Gift! O Holiness!
You raze my heart—
    and bring joyfulness!
Does peace ensue?
    What You embue
Is more than this,
    but blissfulness…
In earthly terms,
    in other words…
Quite extraordinary blooms
    from fatigue and pain;
Another world…
    that opens beyond
This mortal gate
    and sees right through
(And, yes, I'm fond)
    To see Your Face…

If mankind knew
Just how this LOVE
No fortunes blew
And bestowed from above…
Is there for each,
Tho contracts breach,
They'd love like this…
In real whole-ness.

January 21, 2007
Third Sunday in Ordinary Time

O Precious Lord, my true blessedness…
Take my impatience and let it flower…
That I know each kindly act is service
To You, dear Jesus. The total power
Of these deeds of grace brings Christ
To those who are Christ to me…
Through human weakness bright
Rays are cast which salve the need
And dim the shadow. We so can't do
Anything ourselves—but for You
Alone we would lurk and cower…
Divinity is ours to have—Your Substance,
O God, is freely-given. We sacrifice thanks
To You, and in this gift understand
Your LOVE… Union with You created
In this "ordinary" manner elevates
As surely as the most "mystic moment."
For gratitude, Jesus, keeps me growing
In Divine Love—The Holy Spirit…
O Creator, never keep me from it…
(If this is where impatience went…)

Friday, February 2, 2007
PRESENTATION OF OUR LORD

O Christ, my Lord, my praise pours forth…
My life of sin is hardly worth
Your cross or hope of heaven's berth,
But love prevails in mercy's search…

And if You were to give me more,
Just what it'd be—would make me soar…
To heaven's reach beyond all pain…
And You I'd gain! I'd see Your Face!

You'd make me You! You'd give
Me peace—and joy and love to live
Always. With You my breath
Would never cease…we'd breathe
Out LOVE—eternally…

So give me grace to tell the world
The words of Love that You've unfurled
In harmony. So I can sing Your praises
To this world with wings…

O Majesty, I come today, somewhat forlorn…
    a little late…
But by Your leave, I take a place…
    by Your gate…
Next to heaven's peace.

For You are here—in splendor near.
With friends abide, right at my side...
In unity with One-Yet-Three...
We all will be this Mystery...

O Joy of Peace and Happiness!
This perfect bliss is heaven's gift!
O God You give me all of this.
In awesome LOVE—never finishes!

Friday, February 2, 2007
The Presentation of Our Lord

"My God, my God, why have You abandoned me!"
Cried Jesus from the cross as Divine Identity was lost...
This most acute agony—this bitter cup—no blasphemy,
Was felt so intensely by His tender human heart...
And we, accustomed to God's loving Presence;
Acquainted with God's customs know God tests us.
Perhaps we know the trials of this great denial...
Yet we also know its blessings... In God's style
We look to see the "others"—the ones who
Never felt God's loving, or the ones who through
Their hearts' hardness reject it, or even worse hate
It. In our abundance we feel sorrow—so great
Affliction almost "sets in." Our own soft souls
Are bleeding tears for this humankind whose goal
Is not that of possessing LOVE beyond all LOVE.
This lets me consider just where "is the rub"...
And then I wonder if "being possessed" by Someone
Holds fear? Perhaps for few, freedom
Seems an issue... Education plays a role
Here—so I will expound for these intrepid souls,
But that is for another day, another poem...
I will leave well enough now for now alone.

Saturday, February 3, 2007
St. Blase

In front of the Blessed Sacrament...

I've always known—when here like this—
Before the host—Blessed Sacrament...
The world is altered, and I'm in bliss;
And it's no hoax...it's heaven-sent.

O You, dear Jesus—my hope, my life...
For You I share that cross of wood and strife.
For You Who gave in poverty like me
More LOVE than can be fathomed or be seen.

No agony is too much to endure—
For You are there—all ills to cure
With happiness beyond earth's knowing...
A spirit's fulfillment—in the bread showing.

So come with me—O Holy Spirit
From this blessed place, if so I merit...
And rest with me—in unity...
With all this parish—as God wills it to be.

February 6, 2007
SS Paul Miki and Companions

Composed in front of the Blessed Sacrament...while thinking of
that same "song" that has so hounded me lately...

Dearest One, You taught me how
Your abundant gifts convert
To naught... It is in me—when pride
And greed turn sour Your works...
Then for me—it's misery...

Today at church I saw a need...
A "little one" approached and pleaded
"Some money to spare?"...and, of course, I cared...
So I handed over, everything to her.

And in my prayer this little one
Came to mind—I wasn't blind
To my generosity—which is the key—
I started to think...like an addiction to drink.

My prayer was distracted—by thoughts of riches...
And where this went—my prayer was spent...
On even more, bigger debts and stores...
Thoughts of money grew—and how I then stewed...

But then I knew—I am weak without You...
This one encounter—though it was disaster!
Shows me how we humans—so weak and fragile!
Need Your guiding hand—so we safely land!

February 9, 2007
Friday of the 5th Week in OT

Perfectly… You do it just perfectly,
My Lord, and My God. Your Word,
Your Gifts—life, trials and crosses, free
Choices, passions, meanings—complex and meaty…
Lord, all these are considered "Providence" to me—
And are richness. To assure You—
Your gifts enormous bring union—
But only as my friends think through
The delicate mercies each gift's communion
Wrought exquisite, infinite in glory…
Even though quite ordinary-appearing
To earthly eyes unaccustomed to stories
Of mystic harmonies which You bring
Quietly, yeah, silently on angel's wings
To those of us who wait for them.
Open these blind eyes, dear One, to when
Your gifts are given—ALWAYS
    and for the remaining days…
Let them know Your tenderness
    and caring ways…
That Your gifts are profound
    and abundant LOVE-sweets
        until heaven greets…
O Blessed and Monumental Gifter of Mercies…
I love THEE eternally!

February 9, 2007
Friday of the 5th Week of OT

Sometimes
The Lord hides…
And you can't find
No matter how hard you try—
No matter how wide
You open your eyes.

You stumble, you fall…
And that isn't all…
Almost give up
(from this cup we sip)
Humankind "slips."

These are the ways of God…
By these trials we are taught;
And these struggles are fraught,
Believe it or not,
With fearsome passions rendered
So our love is tendered.

God brings us to our knees—
Surrendering what is "me"…
To give it all to the One
Who reigns as Father/Son
And Holy Ghost like none
Who ever IS, Was, or Will BE…
Holy, Holy, Holy! Amen…

February 9, 2007
Friday of the 5th Week of OT

The rose window above the altar and Blessed Sacrament at the church in Bremerton, Washington is so incredibly beautiful...particularly in the early morning, when I go to adore...

I kneel beneath the altar to pray;
Head bowed in humble thanks and praise...
Before the Blessed Sacrament I lay
All my faults and cares today. Then I gaze
Above the crucifix—which in darkness
Hides the magnificent—a stained
Glass portrait of sheer Holiness...
The Lamb of God now waiting silently.
Heaven's comfort descends quietly
Upon me—contemplation's gift... Peace
To be my best. This, God's blessing
In my fatigue, relieves all my pain.
Night-time's blackness begins uncovering
As the day commences. I look to see
The window—now bathed in lively light—
And lo! The Lamb of God appears! Be
Certain it is He! For the Sun so bright
It blinds us—and the radiance we feel!
The Unknowable now known to us
And our senses served to tell...
But it is our hearts that really show
For they were made for God to fill...
Now gone are all our cares and woes—

For here is Jesus to do God's Will...
That humans know God understands
Human poverty, human suffering...
Human violence unto death He went; grand
The vision is—facts not buffering...
Truth is telling here (my tears are welling near...)
And yet He rose from death—for the victory—
Which is ours today, is our future's glory...
So needs of all us mortal humankind
Be fulfilled far beyond all imagining—
To eternity all Love, Truth, and Beauty...
Amen, Amen, Amen...

February 9, 2007
Friday of the 5th Week of OT

It was as though I finally saw…
A world apart—where man can't walk…
Where spirits dwell. O Sovereign Power—
Are souls kept there? I couldn't knock…
It seemed to be (to little me) a vision clear…
Not a dream—I'm wide awake! Unlock
The secret of this clarion scene! For it
Calls to me over books of words. Quest
Of being—quest of holiness—allow my spirit
Freedom only to surrender unto God… Guest
Of no world but my Loving Lord—I fear it,
Yes, Dear One, being separate
From You. You promised it…
To us—being All-in-All…
It's what I long…
And where I belong…
To You alone—
The only ONE…
To You I run…
My God.

February 10, 2007
St. Scholastica

Not long ago I wrote a poem wondering if persons who don't
pursue "Love Beyond All Love" did so because they were afraid
of "being possessed." So I write this one now...

God's Freedom...

A relationship with God is one of LOVE—
At least in Christianity (because that's what Jesus said).
One COULD say one is "possessed by God"
I suppose; but just as much (and in laud)
One possesses God... In love relations
There are duties, surely. And in that station
One does duties because one WANTS to do
Them... (because LOVE motivates.) It's strange
Just how freeing LOVE is—one's heart gains
Strength and joy...wants to sing and shout
Because life has new meaning—now seeming
Full of hope. Sing it strong! Sing it LOUD!
Its fullness progresses all the way to eternity!
It is promised and is a covenant (a contract.)
Even in contracts there is liberty. Take back
Your old ideas! This contract ensures
Your freedom forever! Your can choose yours
Today—at this very moment by bowing your head
And surrendering yourself to perfect LOVE
                              (Almighty God!)
And by Jesus be led...

February 10, 2007
St. Scholastica

Dear, dear Jesus, All-Knowing, All-Wise,
You, Who are Bread; You, Who are Wine—
That I consume You make me Thine...
And with my brothers and sisters signed
As ONE beyond all knowledge
Of how this could be... Thankfully
I, humble sometimes being, do not need solid
Evidence of the why of this.
It is enough to know that it exists...
And with it my heart laughs and sings—
Oh, what blissfulness this brings!
For now my very cells are stuff
And substance of my love, Jesus!
I know it very well!
So ring those bells, my friend; I know well!
Come, Jesus! Enter into me right now!
I am here and waiting if You will allow...
Know-well!

February 12, 2007
Monday of the 6th Week of OT

Early morning prayer before the Blessed Sacrament…

In the early morning I run to Thee…
Yet sitting quietly…and waiting expectantly…
In the background I hear murmuring…
Fervent whispering of the loved ones who sing
To Thee in their prayers. Thou art here
Among us welcoming—oh, so warmly,
Oh, so comforting. I see Thy Presence there
In the tabernacle—by the altar—held
In grandeur both for our eyes to feast
And our hearts to bear. But we weld
Lord, as we consume Thee—at least
We become Thee as our very cells meld…
And remembering this sweet communion
Locks me with these friends near in tight union.
So my prayers to Thee are living moments
Soaring toward these… (my heart is stolen…)
And as I listen, Lord, to Thee and them whisper,
Pain and restlessness surcease, and I remember…
Although the darkness of these morning hours
Surrounds us in dimness—light is pervading—bowers
Of hope and love enfold the pray-ers who kneel
Before the Blessed Sacrament before dawn. So seal
Us with Your Knowledge and Mystery
For Thou art nearer yet than our souls can fathom…
Thou art seated on a seat elaborate…
As the simple cell of a human body.

Seemingly so simple—but not—
Artfully complex…
Artfully elegant…
Brimming with PRESENCE!

February 14, 2007
SS Cyril, Monk, Methodius

I was struck this morning at church by the prayer book—one side of the book is for intentions...the other for "thanksgiving. The side for requests and intentions is always very, very full...the side for thanks is often much less full—and today it was empty. My own needs often overcome me, so I am aware of how needy we fragile humans are—and are meant to be. Yet when we are grateful and aware of God's mercies and abundances—even when in crisis and "poverty"—we are truly "in union" with Jesus...

Seized...

Pierced...

Overcome...

Immolated...

To Thee I run
As though devastated
By my attempts to win
My own way—my own life...

But my very works—strive...
Which You know as "pride,"
O Lord, and sin lurks.

EVERYTHING MUST BE YOURS!

This impoverishment makes me free
To be centered in Thee...
What riches in store
Are there and more!

What gravity—
In divinity!
These promises...
Draw me.
Closely I hear
Until You appear—
For awhile there is union...
(glorious communion!)
But I am human—
And must wait until I die
To see Your very eyes...
Yes, I life despise...
For I keep me from Thee—
Most unworthily.
You would have me be—
Blissful beyond measure...
So You gift me heartily
With earthly treasures.
It is now up to me—
To find them and "to see"...
And give You back thankfully
PRAISE!

February 16, 2007
Friday of the 6th Week of OT

The 23rd Psalm Re-written…

My Good Shepherd feeds and leads
Me through ALL life's exciting passages…
And not only that… He tends and guides
Each second of every day… But the way
Isn't wide—rocks and streams are strewn
Just everywhere…to be prepared
To be taken there (in the dark)—
And the dark, too, is…fair…
Because He cares—and is at my side.
He is ALL and has ALL we need…
That is our call when we believe—
In it is true strength, a firm foundation.
This is grace for all God's nations.
So let God bring you this comfort, too!
God created you to need Higher Authority…
When we rebel—it brings out anger. We
Serve ourselves instead of one another.
When I dwell with God, goodness follows,
As surely as anything exists—when I give laud—
God allows an anointing of Spirit
Which fills me with peace and love.
This abundance of table and overflowing cup
Are God's mercies and gifts to us.
For God means for us to be joyful—
To pasture in heaven's bliss always and forever.
Alleluia…

March 8, 2007
Thursday of the 3rd Week of Lent

This was written one early morning meditating while watching
the Columbia River out the window of my brother's home…

The mist lifts off the river
   like incense off the altar of our God…
And my heart sings praises to deliver
   wafting upward toward heaven: laud…
And inward to my soul—the seat of the King
Guarded by the angelic hosts so no one
May provoke this most sacred wellspring
Of humankind's own divinity. For it belongs
To eternity…past all mysterious knowledge…
Past all time and worldly material…
Past all that can be considered certain and solid.
Light flows around—those veiled trees become surreal
Projections knifing into the fog-filled sky…
My own faith-filled core erupts into ecstasy
In wonder and love; lost forever is "why?"
I'm caught in peace and security,
Beyond all certainty…
Two birds glide by
Going Somewhere—it matters not (except to them).
For this, I deeply sigh,
Locked in love I watch daylight break…
The night-time fade…
The world awake…
Slumber forsake…

The river lumbers onward—
For others to be so seized…

April 3, 2007
Tuesday of Holy Week

Breathe me, Eternity...
Now I enter sacred journey
Beyond the clasp
Of reality...
Into full blissfulness—
Your true intention
For ALL humanity.
This Mystery
Ever-seeking...
For delivery
Into God's Kingdom
Where peacefulness
Resides with unity
With the Holy One—
Which pursues us
Endlessly...
Will you give in to it?
And look in silence
Through darkest night...
To greet with meek laughs of joy
This LOVE DIVINE!

Printed in the United States
101603LV00003B/287/A